THE CHRISTIAN ORIENT

The Christian Orient

Published *for*
THE BRITISH LIBRARY

ISBN 0 7141 0666 6

Published by British Museum Publications Ltd.
6 Bedford Square, London WC1B 3RA

 British Library Cataloguing in Publication Data

British Library
The Christian Orient.
1. Near East – Church history –
Exhibitions
I. Title
275.6   BR1070

Designed by John Mitchell

Text set in 10pt Linotron Times
and printed by
G. A. Pindar and Son Ltd, Scarborough.

Plates printed by
Balding and Mansell Ltd,
Wisbech and London.

Contents

THE PLATES
following page 80

MAPS

Preface

THIS introduction to the ancient Christian Churches of the East is based upon materials assembled for exhibition in the King's Library in the British Library from July to September 1978. Greek Christianity and the related Orthodox Churches of Eastern Europe and Georgia are included, as well as the Syriac (both Jacobite and Nestorian), Christian Arabic, Coptic, Nubian, Ethiopic and Armenian. The manuscripts and objects relating to Christian life and worship were made available by the Departments of Manuscripts, and of Oriental Manuscripts and Printed Books, of the British Library; by the Departments of Egyptian Antiquities, Oriental Antiquities, and Medieval and Later Antiquities, of the British Museum; some manuscripts were loaned by the Bodleian Library, Oxford, and the Chester Beatty Library, Dublin, and a book by the British and Foreign Bible Society. The splendid gift of a Khachkar, or Armenian stone cross, was made by His Holiness, Vasken I, Catholicos of all Armenian, for display in the exhibition, and subsequent inclusion in the British Museum collections. To all these, we should like to express our sincere thanks.

I should also like to express special gratitude to all who have contributed materials for the present work: to Dr M. L. Bierbrier, of the Department of Egyptian Antiquities, to Mr R. Camber, formerly of the Department of Medieval and Later Antiquities, and Dr R. Whitfield of the Department of Oriental Antiquities, who provided descriptions of items loaned from their departments of the British Museum; to Mr D. H. Turner of the Department of Manuscripts, British Library, for the section on the Orthodox church and following descriptions, and to Professor D. M. Lang, of the School of Oriental and African Studies, University of London, for the section on Christianity in Georgia; and to members of the Department of Oriental Manuscripts and Printed Books for contributions towards various sections: Mr K. B. Gardner (Oriental Christian Manuscript Bindings); the Revd Dr V. Nersessian (Armenian); Mr E. Silver (Syriac, Coptic, Nubian, Ethiopic), and Dr G. R. Smith (Arabic).

G. E. MARRISON
Director and Keeper
Department of Oriental Manuscripts
and Printed Books

1

Introduction

THE Christian Orient is a term which has been widely accepted as referring to the ancient Churches of the Middle East who have preserved their traditions of worship and fellowship, literature, architecture and art from the earliest times until the present day, even where the lands in which they dwell have been dominated by other civilizations in the course of the centuries.

A matter of key interest is the relationship between the Orthodox tradition and that of other Oriental Christians where there were important mutual influences despite some doctrinal differences. This can be seen when manuscripts representing the Greek tradition, including examples from Constantinople and the other Greek centres, Slav Churches and the Georgian are set side by side with scriptures, liturgies and other texts in Syriac, representing both the Jacobite and Nestorian traditions, Christian Arabic, Coptic, Nubian, Ethiopic and Armenian. The British Library collections are rich in the literatures of many of these Churches and include some splendidly illuminated manuscripts among them. These have been supplemented here by fine examples from the collections of the Bodleian Library, Oxford, and the Chester Beatty Library, Dublin, as well as by a selection of objects relating to Christian life and worship from the British Museum.

The interest we believe that this survey will elicit is first the recognition of many familiar artistic themes, including Old Testament scenes, episodes from the life of Christ and of the Blessed Virgin Mary, portraits of the Evangelists and scenes from the lives of the Saints, in styles different from the tradition of Western Europe; secondly, a comparison among the artistic styles of the various Churches represented. We have not tried to suggest the exact relation of mutual influence between Byzantine painting and that of the other Eastern Churches. Undoubtedly these influences did not all flow in one direction, but the evidence of the items themselves will show the closeness of their development which persisted over the centuries even when there were critical theological differences among the various communions.

Hugo Buchtal and Otto Kurz, the authors of the *Handlist of Illuminated Oriental Christian Manuscripts* alluded to this question at the outset of their work:

9

'The outstanding problem which concerned other historians of Byzantine art is that of the persistency of the Hellenistic tradition on the one hand and the influence of Near Eastern non-Greek art in Christian painting on the other. The classical tendency in Byzantine art is generally described as the survival of late Hellenism; the Oriental influence is regarded as being due to the art of early Christian Syria, Armenia and Egypt. But whereas the architecture of Eastern Christianity has been thoroughly studied, research on the subject of illumination of manuscripts written in the national languages of the Eastern Churches outside Europe has generally been confined to very few examples'.

A good number of the manuscripts referred to by Buchtal and Kurz have been included here and although we would ourselves not offer a solution to the problem of their research, the examples now shown should help in that study. They, however, brought their discussion down only to the fall of Constantinople in 1453 and omitted reference to later materials where the artistic traditions continued in the various Churches but often with new developments, and these too are represented here.

The illuminated manuscript, however, was not an end in itself, but rather a product of the piety and artistic inspiration of a believing community; it served as an adjunct to the holy texts which in their turn had their proper use in the conduct of Christian worship. It is a fact that most of the literatures here represented were very largely Christian in content. Theological writings were wide ranging, but at the centre of all were the scriptures, liturgies, prayer books, hymn books and lives of the Saints. It was these which were needed by ruler and people, by bishop, priest, monk and layman alike for their devotions and it was these which were accorded special attention in the beauty of the scripts in which they were written and in the decoration and illumination which often accompanied them.

The inheritance, both literary and artistic, was a complex one in which the Jewish and wider Semitic background of primitive Christianity played a key part. Equally, the inheritance of the Hellenistic world, including the art and learning of that tradition promoted both in Egypt and Syria, made its contribution. We note here that one of the effects of St Paul's missionary labours was to bring the Jewish and Hellenistic elements of current civilizations together and provide a basis upon which the new Christian culture could develop.

The two most ancient patriarchates of the East were Antioch and Alexandria, both centres of Hellenistic culture, but representing different emphases in their view of the world and consequently of their synthesis of Christian doctrine. These were later to issue in the great Christological controversies of the fourth and fifth centuries AD. In the meanwhile, at the beginning of the fourth century Jerusalem acquired a new importance with the visit of St Helena, mother of Constantine, in AD 326 to venerate the holy places. Shortly afterwards Constantinople became the capital of the Empire and by the middle of the fifth century its Bishop had acquired patriarchal dignity, but not without controversy with the earlier Eastern Churches. Meanwhile the Armenians were the first nation to adopt Christianity officially at the beginning of the fourth century, and the Georgians were evangelised by St Nino slightly later.

Among the early Councils of the Church the most critical for the later history of Eastern Christianity were those of Ephesus, held in 431, at which Nestorianism was condemned and from which time the distinctive character of Eastern Syriac Christianity can be said to have been established. At the Council of Chalcedon (just across the Bosphorus from Constantinople) in 451 the Monophysites, or those who believed in the one nature of Christ, were condemned, the jurisdiction of Constantinople was asserted and the division of Christendom into five Patriarchates was made: Rome, Constantinople, Alexandria, Antioch and Jerusalem. This breach between the Orthodox and Monophysite Churches, although it was strongly defended on theological grounds on both sides, was greatly reinforced by the political rivalries of the various centres concerned. It is from this time that the more distinctively national characteristics became apparent. The Copts in Egypt and the Ethiopians who were closely related with them, both adopted the Monophysite doctrine, as did the Western Syrians, later to be known as Jacobites. The Armenians, busy fighting the Persians, had not been represented at Chalcedon and never recognised its authority, though they do not claim so unambiguously to be bound by the Monophysite position. The Georgians also broke their relationship with Byzantium after Chalcedon, but resumed it in 607 and became an autocephalous Orthodox Church, as were the later Slav Churches.

The later development of Byzantium and the Orthodox Churches is discussed in Chapter 2. For them, as for the Oriental Churches, the rise of Islam was one of the cataclysmic experiences in their later history. The Prophet Muhammed began his preaching in Mecca about AD 610 and from then until his death in 632 consolidated his position in Arabia, the base of subsequent theocratic imperial expansion from which the Christian countries of the Middle East were overrun by 641. In subsequent centuries the Christian Churches of the region maintained their existence, but precariously as tolerated minorities within the Islamic dominions. It became the policy of the Caliphate to recognise the heads of the various Churches as the civil leaders of their communities for whom they were answerable to the Islamic powers. Christian polity was engaged in maintenance of the faith and integrity of the community in these restrictive conditions, and this situation shaped much of their subsequent psychology and history.

The western view of Islam in the ancient centres of Christianity was a very different one, of confrontation rather than adaptation, and resulted in the Crusades from the end of the eleventh to the end of the thirteenth centuries, which finally failed in their objective of freeing the holy places, but also were a major factor in the estrangement between Eastern and Western Christians. The final critical fact in this story was the fall of Constantinople to the Turks in 1453.

For all the diversity of history and temperament which characterises the Churches of the East, there is some degree of common tradition which is seen in their style of teaching, worship and artistic expression, which also differentiate them from the developments in Western Christianity. There are, naturally, aspects of divergence in architectural style among the Oriental Churches, but in the liturgy and its physical, musical and artistic setting there are many points of resemblance in the practice of the Churches even when far apart geographically or of different theological allegiances.

The Icon, which characterizes Eastern Christianity and developed out of the compromise solution following the Iconoclastic controversy of the eighth and ninth centuries, is a shared tradition in these Churches and closely relates to the development of manuscript illumination.

Similarly, the form taken by the book in the service of the Churches, whether scriptures, liturgies, prayers or lives of the Saints, is one in which there are many points of common development throughout the region – the successive use of papyrus, parchment and paper; the development of the Codex as the standard form; advances in leather bookbinding, in which the Coptic tradition in Egypt was pre-eminent in the production of fine tooled bindings – all these reveal parallels from the various sources. Even more important comparisons can be made of the manner in which these books were decorated: there are the Canon Tables, with their characteristic arcaded frameworks; the portraits of the Evangelists which precede the Gospels; the decorated headings which begin the various books of the Bible; ornate initials, illustrations in the margins of texts, and full page miniatures illustrating the Life of Christ, and of his Mother and the Saints, and other similar themes.

Moreover, it is not only in the choice of subject matter, but in the details of presentation that the similarities are to be found. The exact affinities have in many cases still to be determined, as also the direction in which the influences travelled – probably both ways – but the items here described well illustrate the complexity and fascination of this aspect of the subject.

What, however, comes out equally strongly is the overall unity of purpose and even of interpretation, and a considerable consensus as to what is important to represent artistically of the Christian message, which may perhaps best be summed up in the words of St Vincent of Lerins:

Quod ubique, quod semper, quod ab omnibus creditum est:
What has been believed everywhere, always, and by all.

2

The Orthodox Church

THERE are those who consider that by becoming the established religion of the Roman empire Christianity lost more than she gained, even was perverted. This is a superficial opinion. All faiths are presented with a challenge by society. Indeed they originate as a challenge to society and grow initially by questioning and opposing social conventions and niceties. Relentless opposition is however negative and self destructive. Society is only an aggregate of individuals and when enough individuals in a society have been converted, a faith finds that it has become inevitably the new conscience of that society. Further development is possible only by accepting this *rôle*, by adopting the society. This has another inevitable consequence, that the society will survive in part at least in the institutions and visible form of the faith. Whether this survival becomes inhibiting or conductive is the final and greatest challenge from society to a faith, but an attempt to eradicate the survival is suicidal. The Roman Empire is alive today in the traditions of the branch of Christianity known as the Orthodox church, a church which makes continuing tradition her touchstone, in distinction to the Catholic's reliance on papal authority and the Protestant's on the word of scripture.

On 11 May AD 330 the Emperor Constantine the Great solemnly inaugurated a new capital for the Roman empire. Its site was the ancient Greek colony of Byzantium, on the shores of the Bosphorus, at a perfect meeting point between Europe and Asia. Officially Byzantium became New Rome. It was also called Constantinople after its refounder and did not lose its old name. A great deal of ink has been spent over Constantine's attitude to Christianity, but the fact remains that, although he was only baptised on his death-bed, his Christian sympathies amount to a conversion which entrained that of his empire. This was not imposed *en masse*, as happened in Russia in 988, it was relatively gradual. Nevertheless, Constantinople was a Christian foundation. Its local church, as that of the capital of the Christian Roman empire down to its termination with the capture of Constantinople by the Turks on 29 May 1453, naturally grew in preponderance. In 381 an Oecumenical, that is, Universal Council of the church declared the church of Constantinople to be equal in seniority to the church of Old Rome. A similar council in 451 gave the bishop of Constan-

13

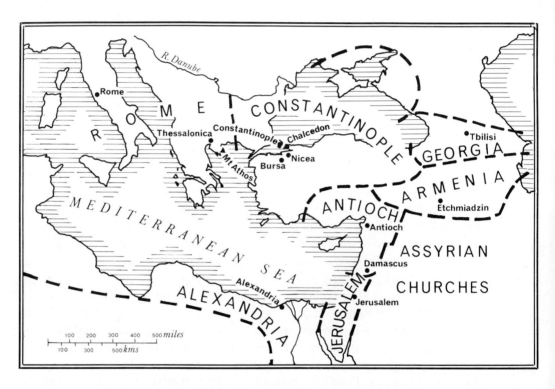

1 *The five ancient Patriarchates, and Georgia, Armenia and Assyria.*

tinople superior jurisdiction over a region roughly comprising the east Balkans and Asia Minor and any churches missionized from there. In the sixth century the term patriarch appears for the heads of what were considered the chief Christian communities, namely those of Rome, Constantinople, Alexandria, Antioch, and Jerusalem. In 588 Patriarch John IV of Constantinople, whose ascetiscism earned him the name of the Faster, scandalized Rome by styling himself Oecumenical Patriarch. His successors enjoy the title to this day.

In the fourth and fifth centuries the Roman empire broke up into western and eastern parts. The western formally ceased to exist in 475. What is known to history as the Holy Roman Empire, beginning in 800, was a recreation of the western part by non-Roman immigrants, originally invaders. Although it tried to be, it was certainly not the lineal heir to the civilization of ancient Greece and Rome. The regime centering on Constantinople was, and never forgot the fact, and also prided itself on having bettered its inheritance by christianizing it. Hence arose the great divide between western and eastern Christianity, in which the chief partisans of the former acquired the epithet Catholic and those of the latter Orthodox. What really sundered them was the Crusades.

Previously the churches of Rome and Constantinople had not been without their differences, but the old idea that they finally broke off relations in 1054 is a myth. From the fourth to the seventh centuries the whole Christian church was troubled by arguments about the precise form of the incarnation of the godhead in Jesus of Nazareth. These resulted in the effective separation of the partriarchates of Alexandria and Antioch from Rome and Constantinople, for political reasons of opposition to the eastern emperors as well as for theological considerations.

When in the seventh century the regions of Alexandria and Antioch fell into Moslem hands, the conquerors found it useful to foster the separation and although patriarchs of Alexandria and Antioch survive who are in communion with Constantinople, they and their adherents are called 'melchites', imperialists. From about 725 to 843 the Byzantine empire was at loggerheads about whether figural representation was permissible in religious art. The victory of the opponents of the practice, the Iconoclasts, would have reduced not only Christian art, but Christianity herself, to symbolism. Luckily they did not prevail. During the controversies about the incarnation and icons relations between the churches of Rome and Constantinople were frequently strained, even severed on occasions. Matters became worse after the Holy Roman Empire had come into being, in favour first of Franks, afterwards of Germans. Further, in the ninth century east and west started a politico-religious squabble over evangelization of the Slavs. The Byzantines won in the main and Christian Slavs were to become an important element in the Orthodox church, almost an overwhelming one after 1453, with Moscow aggrandizing herself as 'the Third Rome'.

Linguistic differences and attitudes were fundamental to the split between

Catholic and Orthodox. The world of early Christianity spoke Greek as its civilized tongue and the basic Christian writings are in Greek. The British Library is the honoured custodian of the second oldest and second most important Greek bible, the Codex Sinaiticus, so called because of its discovery at the monastery of St Catherine on Mount Sinai. It dates from the mid-fourth century and is on view in the Manuscripts Saloon. The language of the church at Rome was Greek till the third century. Then Latin took its place and became the medium of west European culture. Whilst Catholicism is essentially Latin and Orthodoxy essentially Greek, Greek never assumed the exclusivity for the latter that Latin did for the former. This was because of the survival of the Roman empire, which was an amalgam of cultures, as the vehicle of Orthodox Christianity, which always admitted worship in the vernacular. Thus, the brothers Sts Cyril and Methodius, the apostles of the Slavs, created for their converts Church Slavonic, which is still in use, from the dialect of the Slavs in the suburbs of their home town of Thessalonica. By then, the ninth century, liturgies in Armenian, Coptic, Syriac, Georgian, and other languages existed in eastern Christianity and future translations included Romanian in the seventeenth century, Japanese in the nineteenth, and English in the twentieth. Of the seventeen manuscripts illustrating the Orthodox church which are described below, thirteen have Greek texts, three Slavonic, and one Romanian.

By 1054 Latin west and Greek east had drifted fairly far apart, but the events then were really a personal clash between a tactless and arrogant papal envoy, Cardinal Humbert, and the patriarch of Constantinople, Michael Cerularius, a politician who had had ambitions of the imperial throne, but had had to be content with the patriarchal staff. The Orthodox patriarchs of Alexandria, Antioch, and Jerusalem did not regard themselves as affected by the dispute. In 1095 the First Crusade was launched by Pope Urban II.

The Byzantine emperors had indeed expressed interest in mercenaries from the west, but the onus for two centuries of militarist and ideological expansion by western Europe in the Near East must rest on the papacy. Disguised as a holy war against Islam for the holy places of Christianity the Crusades were really a demonstration by the newly emerging western civilization against the aristocratic hyper-culture of the eastern Mediterranean, Christian as well as Moslem. The result is epitomized in the famous remark attributed to the Byzantine high admiral, Luke Notaras, in 1453 that he would rather see a Turk's turban in St Sophia's, the cathedral of Constantinople, than a cardinal's hat. Already in about 1200 a Byzantine historian wrote, 'Between us and the Latins is set the widest gulf', and in 1204 the Fourth Crusade sacked Constantinople, where a civil and ecclesiastical government from the Latin west ruled till 1261. The period is known as the Latin empire. The restored Greek empire was no longer a great power, but 1261 to 1453 saw Byzantine, that is, Orthodox, thought and art reach their apogee.

16

The Israelites led by Moses and Aaron. Stoudion Psalter. Greek, AD 1066.
Add.19352, f.99b. (Cat. No. 4)

Christ's Entry into Jerusalem. Jacobite Gospel Lectionary. Syriac, AD *1216–20.*
Add.7170, f.115a (Cat. No. 29)

There was no juridical breach between Catholic and Orthodox, but by 1261 it was *de facto*. Political considerations induced the eastern Emperors Michael VIII and John VIII to compel union between Constantinople and Rome in 1274 and 1439, but their efforts foundered on popular opposition. After the Sultan Mahomet II conquered Constantinople all Orthodox Christians in the Turkish dominions were placed under the jurisdiction, civil and religious, of the patriarchs of Constantinople.

Save in Russia, where the bishopric of Moscow was raised to the dignity of a patriarchate in 1589, but where from 1721 to 1917 the church was outwardly reduced to a branch of the civil service, the Orthodox church was now a minority group. She became increasingly nationalistic and defensive. *Vis-à-vis* the west she was faced with the Reformation and the Counter-Reformation. A patriarch of Constantinople, Cyril Loukaris, adopted Calvinism. He it was who in 1627 presented to King Charles I of England the Codex Alexandrinus, a Bible in Greek written probably in Egypt in the first half of the fifth century, which is the next earliest and most important manuscript of the Bible after the Codex Sinaiticus. Now in the British Library and on view in the Manuscripts Saloon, the Alexandrinus is so-called because it used to be in the library of the patriarchate of Alexandria, which See Loukaris had previously occupied. Loukaris was answered by Peter Moghila, who became metropolitan of Kiev in 1632, but whose own position was one of uncritical acceptance of contemporary Catholicism. Not till the mid-nineteenth century did Orthodox thought resume its own line.

The Tsarist and Turkish hegemonies led to a polarization of Orthodoxy into Greek and Slav. This was worsened because the church of Constantinople, encouraged by the Turks, tried to gain control of other branches of the Orthodox church, both ancient self-governing ones, like the patriarchates of Alexandria and Antioch, and newer ones, and Grecianize them. Thus, the independence of the churches of Serbia and Bulgaria was suppressed in 1766 and 1767 respectively. In like spirit Russia subjugated the Georgian church in 1817, sixteen years after she had annexed the land of Georgia. Only relatively recently and by no means readily have Constantinople and Moscow been relaxing their hold on Orthodox Christianity, which in the twentieth century, more than any branch of Christianity, has had to withstand the Communist dogma of the necessary disappearance of religion in the classless society. Greece is the only historically Orthodox country where Orthodoxy has substantial freedom, but there are important Orthodox communities in the New World and Australasia. The future of all religion, however, is concerned less with confrontation with materialism than with assimilation of nuclear physics, which has, quite literally, exploded materialism and classical logic. It could be that Orthodoxy will find this easier than any branch of Christianity will. Though largely conservative at present, her history is far more one of absorption of new ideas than rejection and her view of history is a view of an open process not an enclosed one.

1   Cotton Genesis. Greek, Alexandria (?), sixth century. Paper and vellum, 151 folios (originally 165). Fragmentary. Modern binding. Supposed to have been brought to England from Philippi, in Macedonia, by two Greek bishops, who gave it to King Henry VIII. Queen Elizabeth I presented it to her tutor in Greek, Sir John Fortescue, who gave it to the antiquary Sir Robert Cotton (died 1631), whose library was one of the foundation collections of the British Museum in 1753. The Cottonian library had been damaged by fire in 1731, in which the Genesis suffered severely. In 1796 only 18 fragments could be found, but between 1842 and 1856 a total of 147 were reassembled by Sir Frederic Madden, Keeper of Manuscripts 1837–66. Four others had been removed by the Revd Andrew Gifford, assistant librarian in the Department of Manuscripts from 1756 till his death in 1784. These he bequeathed, with other material, to the Bristol Baptist College, from which they were acquired in 1962.

Cotton MS. Otho B. vi.

Despite its sad condition this illustrated copy of the book of Genesis is one of the greatest of Christian relics. It is thought once to have had 250 pictures, the style of which suggests an origin in Egypt, probably at Alexandria, a famed centre of Hellenism and meeting place for the various cultures of the eastern Mediterranean. In the thirteenth century the manuscript's miniatures were possibly direct models for mosaics in St Mark's, Venice, to which city the manuscript could well have come as loot from the Fourth Crusade's sack of Constantinople, for which the Venetians were mainly responsible.

2   Canon Tables. Greek, Constantinople (?), early seventh century. Vellum, 2 folios. Fragmentary. Formerly inserted into a twelfth century manuscript of the gospels, in Greek, as were No. 8. The gospels, with its insertions, belonged to Anthony Askew (1722–74), physician, classical scholar, and traveller in the Near East. Acquired at the sale of his library in 1785.

Additional MS. 5111, ff. 10–11b (Plate 4)

These two leaves are all that remain of a manuscript of the gospels which must have been one of the most splendid illuminated books ever produced. Canon tables are tables of parallel and unique passages in the four gospels, called canons, devised by Eusebius of Caesarea (born c.260, died c.340), the 'father of church history', biographer and ecclesiastical adviser of Constantine the Great. A full set of canon tables numbers ten and they were a standard part of copies of the scriptures for centuries.

3   Bristol Psalter. Greek, end of tenth century. Paper and vellum, ii+265 folios. 105×93 mm. Bound in dark red stamped leather, sixteenth century. Belonged to the Bristol Baptist College in 1921, from which it was acquired in 1923.

Additional MS. 40731.

The sacred poems known as psalms are a fundamental source of the public and private devotions of Christians. The manuscript belongs to a type of Byzantine psalters specialized by literal or allegorical illustrations of the text in the margin. The type probably originated in an atelier of book-production brought into being by the scholar Photius when patriarch of Constantinople from 858 to 867. There are 104 subjects depicted in the margins of the Bristol Psalter. The stylistic period to which the manuscript's illumination belongs is called the Macedonian, after the name of the dynasty which ruled the Byzantine empire from 867 to 1057.

4   Stoudion   Psalter.   Greek,   Constantinople, Stoudion monastery, 1066. Paper and vellum. 208 folios. 231×198 mm. Modern binding, 1963. Acquired for £75 at Sotheby's, 2 February 1853, at the sale of the library of H. P. Borrell (died 1851), a numismatist, who had been a trader at Smyrna. Borrell is thought to have acquired the manuscript from the library of the archbishop of Chios.

Additional MS. 19352. (Colour Plate I)

This is the most abundantly illustrated of all ten surviving Byzantine 'marginal' psalters, having representations of no less than 460 subjects. It was commissioned by Michael, abbot of the Stoudion monastery, the chief centre of religious life in Constantinople, and written and illuminated by Theodore, one of his monks, a priest and a native of Caesarea, who finished it in February 1066. Stoudion was famed as an atelier of book-production and the psalter is the most important survivor from this. The illustrations show a linearism, which is typical of mid-eleventh century Byzantine painting, and recalls enamelling.

5   Menologion, September Volume. Greek, late eleventh century. Paper and vellum, 273 folios. 420×320 mm. Modern binding. Belonged to Samuel Butler, bishop of Lichfield (died 1839), from whose estate it was acquired, together with 288 other manuscripts, in 1841.

Additional MS. 11870.

Every day the church commemorates one or more events and characters in her history. A menologion is a collection of notices of these happenings and people, and the standard menologion used in the Orthodox church is a compilation by St Simeon Metaphrastes – which means St Simeon the Translator – in the second half of the tenth century. This is one of a number of sumptuous copies of his work, with illustrations, which are extant: in part at least, for no complete illustrated menologion covering the whole twelve months survives.

6 Pantocratoros Gospel-Book. Greek, Constantinople (?), late eleventh century. Paper and vellum, 10+196 folios. 380×280 mm. Bound in blue velvet, with gilt ornaments, seventeenth century. Acquired by the traveller and bibliophile Robert Curzon (died 1873), from Xenophontos monastery on Mount Athos in 1827. Previously belonged to Pantocratoros monastery there. Curzon's manuscripts were bequeathed to the British Museum by his daughter Darea, Baroness Zouche (died 1917).

Additional MS. 39603.

As distinct from a manuscript of the four gospels which contains these in full in their traditional order, a gospel-book, or -lectionary, contains the passages from the gospels which are read in the church's services throughout the year, arranged for this purpose. The Pantocratoros lectionary was probably produced in the imperial scriptorium at Constantinople. It is one of the only three known Byzantine manuscripts written throughout in cruciform format.

7 Gospels. Greek, Constantinople (?), Pantocratoros monastery (?), first quarter of twelfth century. Paper and vellum, 213 folios. 223×177 mm. Modern binding. Belonged to Charles Burney, classical scholar and schoolmaster. After his death in 1817 his books, which included more than eighty manuscripts in Greek, were acquired for £13,500.

Burney MS.19.

There are three chief periods in Byzantine art, the Macedonian (see No. 3), the Comnenan, and the Palaeologan (see No. 11). The miniatures, of the four Evangelists, in this manuscript are fine examples of painting from the time of the emperors of the house of Comneni (1081–1185). The manuscript is one of a closely related group of books, possibly produced in an atelier at the Pantocratoros monastery in Constantinople, founded by Irene, wife of the Emperor John II Comnenus (1118–43).

8 Miniatures of the Evangelists Matthew, Luke and John. Early thirteenth century. Vellum. 335×255 mm. Formerly inserted into the same manuscript as No. 2.
Additional MS. 5111, f. 12; 5112, ff. 3, 134.

(Plate 5)

These three miniatures have been variously dated between the twelfth and fourteenth centuries. Most likely is the early thirteenth, when a wave of classicism affected Byzantine painting in reaction to the mannerism which had manifested itself in the later twelfth.

9 Services for the Consecration of a Church, and Other Rites. Greek, c.1200. Vellum roll, 5 m. 9 mm.×210 mm. From the collection of Robert Curzon (see No. 6).

Additional MS.39584.

The earliest books were in the form of scrolls. What is immediately connotated now by the word book, namely a codex, that is, a series of pages bound together, appeared in the first century after Christ. It did not generally supersede the roll till the fourth century, and the roll survived for certain specialized purposes. Amongst these was not infrequently transcription of the services of the Orthodox church.

10 Gospels. Greek, c.1225. Paper and vellum, 270 folios. 230×165 mm. Modern binding. From the library of Robert Harley, first earl of Oxford (died 1724), and his son Edward, second earl (died 1741), the manuscripts in which were one of the foundation collections of the British Museum.

Harley MS. 1810 (Plate 10)

The period of the manuscript's execution, really that of the Latin empire (1204–61), saw considerable experimentation and development in Byzantine art, which prepared the way for the great efflorescence which was the Palaeologan style (see No. 11). A state in this preparation is seen in the miniatures in the present manuscript. It is a stage in which traditional classicism is refined by a virtually youthful gracefulness.

11 Gospels. Greek, 1285. Paper and vellum, 317 folios. 190×148 mm. Modern binding, 1964. Belonged to Charles Burney (see No. 7).

Burney MS. 20.

This manuscript was written by a monk called Theophilus, who completed his work on Wednesday, 30 May 1285. It contains miniatures of the four Evangelists which demonstrate well Byzantine art during its greatest period, the Palaeologan. This is named after the family of Palaeologi, who provided the imperial dynasty at Constantinople from 1261 to 1453. Palaeologan painting grew to be daringly experimental with form and colour. The result was one of the greatest successes the world has seen in the representation of the highest thought and the highest emotion, and the inevitable tension between such extremes.

12 Gospels. Greek, 1314–15. Paper and vellum, ii+254 folios. 205×155 mm. Original binding of stamped brown leather. Belonged to the Revd John Samuel Dawes, D.D., sometime chaplain on Corfu, from whom, together with eleven other Greek manuscripts, it was acquired in 1904.

Additional MS. 37002.

The manuscript contains miniatures of the four Evangelists which, although not in good condition, are of much interest for the development of the Palaeologan style. The best preserved of them, St Mark, is also unusual compositionally. Representations of the Evangelists are the most frequently found miniatures in Byzantine illuminated manuscripts. Generally they are shown either as standing orators or lectors or as seated authors, most frequently in the latter pose. When seated they are normally in profile, but Mark in the present manuscript is seated frontally, which is very rare.

13 Serres Gospels. Slavonic, Serres, 1354–55. Paper and vellum, ii+302 folios. 320×220 mm. Modern binding. Acquired by Robert Curzon from the monastery of St Paul on Mount Athos in 1837 (see further No. 6).

Additional MS. 39626. (Plate 16)

A note at the end of the manuscript tells how it was written during the reign of Stephen, tsar of Serbia, in the days of his queen Helen and his son Urosh, when Joanicius was the first patriarch of Serbia, for the Metropolitan Jacob of Serres, in the year of the world 6863 (AD 1354–55). Stephen Dushan, who ruled Serbia from 1331–55, proclaimed himself tsar in 1345 and in

the following year raised the archbishopric of Ipek to a patriarchate. Queen Helen was a French princess and Urosh succeeded Dushan, dying in 1371. Dushan made Serres, now in north-eastern Greece, his capital and the Metropolitan Jacob, who is depicted in a miniature in the manuscript, offering it to Christ, was well known as a bibliophile.

14 Gospels of Tsar Ivan Alexander. Slavonic, 1355–56. Paper and vellum, i+283 folios. 330×250 mm. Original binding of stamped scarlet leather, originally jewelled. Acquired by Robert Curzon from the same source as No. 13 (see further No. 6).

Additional MS. 39627.

The most famous surviving book ever produced in Bulgaria is this copy of the four gospels written in 1355–56 by a monk called Simon for Ivan Alexander, tsar of Bulgaria 1331–71. The text is illustrated with 366 miniatures and at the beginning of the manuscript the tsar and his family are portrayed across two facing pages. The textual illustrations are copied from a mid-eleventh century Byzantine manuscript.

15 Gospels. Slavonic, end of fifteenth century. Paper, 315 folios. 205×150 mm. Modern binding. Purchased from V. Ebbesen, a Norwegian diplomat, in 1930.

Egerton MS. 3045.

Russian Orthodox art is dominated by the genius of the painter-monk Andrew Rublev (died c.1427–30), who interpreted the Palaeologan style in an etherealized and elegant manner which has resemblances, possibly direct relations, with contemporary west European art. The miniatures, of the Evangelists in the present manuscript which is of Russian provenance, show the suavity which became typical of Byzantine art in Russia.

16 Radul Gospels. Romanian, 1574. Paper, 276 folios. 200×150 mm. Modern binding. From the Harleian library (see No. 10).

Harley MS. 6311 B.

This is the earliest surviving dated manuscript in the Romanian language. Although Romanian normally uses the Latin alphabet, this text is in Cyrillic characters, that is, the Slavonic alphabet, devised by St Cyril, apostle of the Slavs (see p. 16). The manuscript was written by Radul the Grammarian for John Petrashko, ruler of Walachia.

17 Leitourgikon from Brusa. Greek, Constantinople, 1644. Paper, 60 folios. 225×165 mm. Bound in dark red leather, gilt stamped, 17th century. Acquired in 1939.

Egerton MS. 3155 (Plate 17).

A leitourgikon contains the texts needed by the celebrant at the eucharist in the Orthodox church. As the act of public worship *par excellence* the eucharist is customarily known to the Orthodox as the liturgy. Three standard series of prayers are used at it, called the Liturgies of St John Chrysostom, St Basil the Great, and the Presanctified. The present manuscript was written at Constantinople in 1644 by Michael, treasurer of the diocese of Brusa, in north-western Asia Minor. It has ornamental and figural illumination in a hieratic style which became typical of Greek Orthodox art during the Turkish hegemony.

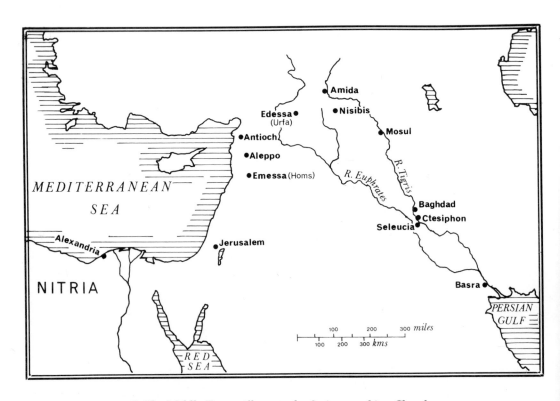

2 *The Middle East to illustrate the Syriac-speaking Churches*

3

The Syriac Speaking Churches and Christian Arabic

ANTIOCH

Antioch was the third city of the Roman empire, and it was here that the Disciples were first called Christians. Local tradition names St Peter as the first bishop; by the beginning of the second century there was a strong Christian community headed by St Ignatius, who was martyred in AD 107.

From the fourth century onwards, Antioch came after Rome and Alexandria as the third patriarchal See, but as Constantinople rose in power so the influence of Antioch began to wane, and this was further weakened by the Nestorian and Monophysite schisms.

Antioch shared with Alexandria the leading place in the early development of Christian theology; sometimes there was agreement, often acute difference between them. In Antioch the approach to the study of the scriptures was historical and critical, and the doctrine of the Holy Trinity was economic, that is, the Three Persons are only differentiated by their manner of operation. These divergencies became more marked in the fifth century, when the great controversies over the nature of Christ arose. With the importance which the Antiochene theologians placed on history, they emphasized the humanity of Christ more than his divine nature.

NESTORIANISM

The teaching of Nestorianism was that there were two distinct persons in the incarnate Christ, one divine and one human, whereas orthodox teaching held that Christ was a single person, both God and man. Consequently the term *theotokos*, or 'bearer of God', which was widely used of the Virgin Mary, was rejected by the Nestorians as contrary to Christ's humanity.

Early in the fifth century, Nestorius became a monk in Antioch, where he both learnt theology, and gained fame as a preacher. In 428 the Roman emperor, Theodosius II, made him Bishop of Constantinople. His chaplain, Anastasius, preached against the use of the term *theotokos*, and Nestorius supported him in this. This led his opponents in Constantinople to seek support from St Cyril, the Patriarch of Alexandria, and the Egyptian monks. The teaching of Nestorius was condemned

23

in Rome by Pope Celestine in 430, and in the following year Nestorius was deposed at the Council of Ephesus.

Those eastern Bishops who had refused to accept this situation formed the nucleus of the Nestorian Church, with its centre in Persia, whose East Syrian Christians had already become independent of Antioch since the Synod of Markatba in 424. A Nestorian theological school was set up at Edessa (Urfa), within the Roman empire, under Bishop Ibas, who had supported Nestorius at the Council of Ephesus. Edessa was famous for its biblical studies, and it was probably here that both the Old Syriac and Peshitta versions of the New Testament were translated. After the Council of Chalcedon in 451, the Monophysites showed their hostility to the Nestorians; many migrated to Persia and in 489 the Emperor Zeno expelled the last of them. A new Nestorian school was founded at Nisibis in 457, under the leadership of Barsumas, a pupil of Ibas, and this now became the leading Nestorian centre.

From 498 the Nestorian Patriarch of the East had his See city at Seleucia-Ctesiphon, the Persian capital of the Tigris. From the sixth century, the Nestorians sent evangelistic missions to Arabia, India and Central Asia. After the Arab conquest of Persia in the middle of the seventh century, the Christians were recognised as a protected minority under their Patriarch, and from 775 he took up his residence at Baghdad. They suffered from the Mongol invasions of the thirteenth century and that of Timur in the fourteenth. Some escaped to the hills in Kurdistan and survived till the present day, and are known as the Assyrian Christians.

THE JACOBITES

The Western Syrians rejected the doctrines propounded at the Council of Chalcedon in 451, for they held that there was a single divine nature in the person of Christ Incarnate and were hence known as Monophysites. However it was in the following century, through the leadership of Jacob Bardaeus (500–578) that they became the national church of Syria, and were later called Jacobites. After the Muslim conquest of Syria from 635, though they received protection, many became Muslims, and in later times numbers declined due to internal factions. At present they are about 200,000, and their Patriarch (of Antioch) has his seat at Homs (the ancient Emesa). Their liturgy, known as the Syriac of St James embodies the Antiochene tradition. They make the sign of the Cross with one finger to reiterate their belief in the single, divine, nature of Christ.

THE MARONITES

This is another Christian Syrian group, who claim origin from St Maro, a friend of St Chrysostom at the beginning of the fifth century. In 1181, during the period of the

Crusades they entered into communion with the Roman Catholic Church, and continue as a uniate body. They are mostly concentrated in the Lebanon. In 1584, a Maronite college was founded in Rome, which gained special fame in the eighteenth century through the work of the scholarly Assemani family, by which Syriac Christian literature became better known in the west.

SYRIAC LANGUAGE AND SCRIPT

Syriac is a dialect of Eastern Aramaic, the one spoken in the early centuries of the Christian era in the principality of Edessa, corresponding to the present day northern Syria and Iraq and southern Turkey. It is written in the same alphabet of 22 consonants as Hebrew, but with characters of its own, which finally developed into three different scripts. The earliest is known as *Estrangela*, characterized by beauty and clarity, as is to be seen in the fifth-century manuscript of the Pentateuch (No. 19), the earliest dated biblical codex, and the nearly contemporary Curetonian Gospels (No. 18), a principal source for the Old Syriac text of the New Testament. This script continued in use until the thirteenth century.

The *Jacobite* script, which was easily written, came into use in the eighth century and was extensively employed till the sixteenth. From the sixth century onwards, a different development of the Estrangela was used by the Nestorians, with a distinctive cursive form in the thirteenth century, which continues in use at the present day.

The devoted labours of missionaries preaching in Syriac caused that language to be diffused through the continent of Asia, while the script was adapted for local use. A striking example of this is the Mongol script, introduced by Nestorian missionaries, and modified for the Mongol language, but turned on its side, so that it is read from top to bottom.

SYRIAC LITERATURE

Syriac literature is wholly Christian, though by no means wholly religious. Busy prelates and persecuted priests, humble deacons and unordained monks, martyrs and hermits, saints and heretics, between them have left us a great quantity of writings, not only on every conceivable theological theme, but also on all the secular subjects known in their time. Unfairly, it has been said that little of their work was original: it is true that the Syrians translated extensively from Greek works; it is also beyond dispute that they taught the Arabs, by translating from Syriac into Arabic, Greek philosophy, logic and grammar, mathematics, astronomy and astrology, natural sciences and medicine, geography and history. They also wrote fiction, biography, bibliography, and works on music and politics, and of humour, among other things.

The earliest Syriac books were biblical translations; these were followed very closely by liturgies, hymns, apocryphal works and theological tracts. Controversy will long continue as to whether one or more of the Gospels was originally composed in Syriac, as well as whether Ephrem the Syrian (306–373) was the inventor of rhyme as a poetic device.

The last Persian war with Byzantium, beginning in 605, wrought havoc among both Jacobites and Nestorians (the best contemporary record of it is in Syriac), and although the Arab conquest soon after brought periods of physical respite and religious tolerance, the Syriac language never fully recovered for, as in Egypt, the Christians learned to speak Arabic and eventually wrote their literature in it.

The thirteenth century saw a final flicker before the end of Syriac as a literary language, with the works of Bar Hebræus, (1226–86), the Jacobite bishop and philosopher. Among his writings, his *Chronicle*, a universal history, contains an account of the Crusade of King Richard I of England.

MANUSCRIPTS

The British Library is fortunate in having one of the world's largest collections of Syriac manuscripts, which is of great interest to scholars, orientalists, theologians, historians and many others; but visually the collection has little to boast. Those Syrian scribes were models of sedulousness, turning out quire after quire of huge, closely-written folios, but they were also dismally puritanical, getting on with the job of putting down their thoughts for posterity, usually in careful, if not beautiful, calligraphy, but rarely with any ornamentation beyond an occasional red and black band between chapters, or an interlaced arch and half-border on the first page.

Notable exceptions are some late lectionaries – books of Gospel readings for feasts, fasts and Sundays of the year. One or two of these even have gold in places; more often an ornamental cross at the beginning or end, coloured tables of the Eusebian Canons, occasionally a single miniature of an Evangelist, or the Virgin and Child, but rarely as many miniatures as in the series of Gospel scenes in No. 29, below.

Some Syriac amulets have been included for comparison with Ethiopic ones (see Nos. 100–103, below). Examples of Syriac manuscript bindings are given at Nos. 150–51.

ARABIC IN CHRISTIAN USE

The Islamic conquest of countries in the Middle East caused Arabic to become the common language in many areas where Syriac had been current, as well as in Coptic-speaking Egypt. Arabic was consequently adopted by the Christians for day to day use, while their ancient languages were retained in the liturgies.

26

Translations were made of the New Testament, the oldest known manuscript being an Arabic translation of the Syriac Peshitta, made in the eighth century. It was not until the thirteenth century, however, that the Churches gave official encouragement to the production of Arabic versions in Alexandria. Arabic Gospels were first printed in Rome in 1591.

The Syrians also adapted their alphabet for writing Arabic; this is called Karshuni and the British Library holds a number of such manuscripts.

18 The Curetonian Gospels. This manuscript contains the Old Syriac version of Matthew, Mark (of which only the end remains), John and Luke. It is copied on vellum in two columns in a fine, bold Estrangela hand of *c*.450–470, without vowel pointing, and with simple punctuation.

Add. 14451. (Plate 3)

This was one of the many Syriac manuscripts brought from Egypt by H. Tattam, from the convent of St Mary Deipara, the so-called Monastery of the Syrians, in the Nitrian Desert, in 1842. These gospels were privately printed by W. Cureton in 1848 and published in 1858; Cureton was on the staff of the British Museum from 1837 to 1849. Three leaves from this manuscript are in Berlin; the only other copy of this version known was from the monastery of St Catherine on Mount Sinai, which was photographed in 1892 and subsequently published. The Old Syriac version of the New Testament was in use before the Peshitta version was prepared in the fifth century and the readings of the Old Syriac are often closed to those of the western text of the Greek New Testament.

19 Pentateuch. This manuscript contains the Peshitta version of Genesis, Exodus, Numbers and Deuteronomy, copied on vellum in a fine bold Estrangela hand, by the deacon John at Amida in 463, and has vowel points added by a later hand; from the Nitrian collection.

Add. 14425. (Plate 2)

This is the earliest known dated Biblical codex. The Peshitta or 'simple' version of the Syriac text became the official translation used by the Syriac speaking Churches in the fifth century. It is believed that the New Testament portion was prepared by Rabbula, Bishop of Edessa from 411 to 435; he ordered copies of the 'Separate Gospels' to be placed in every church, instead of the Diatessaron, or Gospel Harmony of Tatian which had previously been widely used. The place of copying, Amida, was from ancient times a strategic city on the upper Tigris, and the seat of a bishop. The modern town is called Diyarbakir, in eastern Turkey.

20 The Book of Daniel. Peshitta version. This was copied at the Convent of the Orientals, probably Edessa, in 532 in a large regular Estrangela hand, with lessons indicated by rubrication or marginal notes

Add. 14445

The text also contains the Apocryphal portions of Daniel, that is the Song of the Three Holy Children, Bel and the Dragon, and the History of Susanna. Prefixed to this volume is a Table of Lessons for the Book of Proverbs. in a different hand from the main work, perhaps of the eighth or ninth century; this was drawn up by Severus, with the aid of the priest John and the deacon Romanus. The manuscript was one of 250 brought to the convent of St Mary Deipara in the Nitrian Desert in Egypt, by Moses of Nisibis in 932.

21 Deuteronomy and Judges. Peshitta version, copied in a fine, regular Estrangela hand in the sixth century.

Add. 14438.

This manuscript has an interesting initial page, in a different, probably later hand than the main work, in which the Gloria in Excelsis is arranged in the form of a cross, with the opening words of Psalm 91 in an ornamental nimbus: 'He that dwelleth under the defence of the Most High'. Other verses from the Psalms are also given: 'Let God arise, and let his enemies be scattered', (Ps.68.v.1); 'Save me, O God, for thy Name's sake', (Ps.54.v.1.), and 'Have mercy, O God, after thy great goodness', (Ps.51.v.1.).

22 Metrical Discourses of Isaac of Antioch and Others. This manuscript is from the Great Convent of Teleda, and was copied at the end of the sixth century. The text is in two narrow columns, without vowel points and with occasional rubrication. F.151b, at the end of the work has an illuminated cross, with nimbus and border in yellow and green, depicted by Alexander, who was possibly also the copyist.

Add. 14591.

Isaac of Antioch was born in Amida, *c*.365 and educated at Edessa. He went to Rome, and then returned to a convent near Antioch where he died *c*.461. He was a Monophysite, one of the best known Syriac writers, and his homilies, on ascetic and other subjects, are mostly in heptameter verse. This volume also contains some of his hymns, as well as works of other Syriac writers, including Peter of Callinicus, the Jacobite Patriarch of Antioch from 578 to 591.

23 Exodus. Paul of Tella's version, founded on Origen's Hexapla. This was copied by Lazarus on vellum in 697 in a fine regular Estrangela hand. The index of lessons is arranged in three columns of six circles, and the text has marginal notes and glosses, some in Greek.

Add. 12134.

Paul was Bishop of Tella in Syria, and made a translation of the Septuagint in 616–17, following the Hexapla of Origen. This Syriac version enjoyed popularity for a time. The colophon shows the care with which the translator collated his Greek sources.

24 The Books of Samuel. This version is in the recension of Jacob of Edessa. It was copied by Lazarus and Adi on vellum in 719, in a large and beautiful Estrangela hand, with Greek vowel points occasionally added. It contains a table of lessons in circles and arcading.

Add. 14429

Jacob, Bishop of Edessa, was one of the most famous Monophysite scholars at the end of the seventh century. One of the colophons states that the present work was corrected with great care from the Greek and Syriac versions in 705 at the Great Convent of Teleda.

25 Bible Lectionary. Lessons, mostly in the Peshitta version, and according to the Jacobite use, arranged by Athanasius, Patriarch of Antioch. The manuscript was copied by Constantine, in the convent of Barsauma in 1000, in a stiff and formal Estrangela hand, with occasional vowel pointing. At f.57b. there is a marginal illustration of the Annunciation.

Add. 12139.

The text contains 53 sets of lessons for Sundays, feast days and other special occasions, such as for the reception of a bishop, and for services in times of drought, and in public distress. The first set is for the Annunciation, and as in most other cases includes two lessons from the Old Testament and one from the New. For the feast of the Nativity, eight old Testament portions are given, and one New, from Galatians 4: 'The heir as long as he is a child . . .'

26 Gospel Lectionary. The text is in the Philoxenian version, and was copied in the twelfth century. It has a table of lessons, and at ff.4b–5 illustrations of the Nativity, Adoration of the Magi, Christ's Entry into Jerusalem, and the Four Evangelists.

Or. 3372.

Philoxenus (Aksenaya) was born in Persia, studied under Ibas at Edessa, and was made Bishop of Mabbug in 485. He was a Monophysite, and was exiled by the Emperor Justin I in 518 and he died in 523. His writings include commentaries and liturgies. The Philoxenian version of the New Testament was made under his direction by his Chorepiscopus Polycarp, and is noted for its pure and elegant style.

27 Gospel Lectionary. This manuscript, giving lessons according to the Jacobite use, was copied about 1200. The beginning of the volume contains ornate decorated and coloured crosses, tables of lessons in circles and squares, and a series of full-page miniatures of Gospel scenes, beginning with the Nativity and Baptism of Christ. The text is in two columns in bold script with decorated bands and some rubrication.

Add. 7169.

This very large volume has illustrations in formal hieratic style, which nevertheless convey a sense of spirituality. Some of the pictures are diagrammatic, the various figures being shown detached and at different angles. F.11a shows the Last Supper as seen from above a round table. F.247a, at the end of the text, has Jesus shown head and shoulders with a nimbus of red and yellow, surrounded by six saints also in roundels.

28 Psalter. The Psalms according to the Jacobite use in this volume were copied by Shim'un in the convent of St Mary at Beth Ahsenaye on Mount Edessa in 1204. The text is in single column, with rubrications.

Add. 7154.

At the beginning of the volume are a number of miniatures, including at f.1b. the Virgin in purple robe with a halo, holding a curly-headed infant Christ in her arms, his head turned upwards towards his Mother. F.2a. has King David, robed like a medieval monarch, with his harp, and the Temple shown in the background in red outline. The following pages include illustrations of saints in formal, hieratic style.

29 Gospel Lectionary. This gives the lessons in the Philoxenian version, according to the Jacobite use. It was copied on paper in a bold Estrangela hand in two columns, from the monastery of Mar Mattai near Mosul, 1216–20. It contains numerous miniatures with scenes from the life of Christ.

Add. 7170. (Colour Plate II)

This very large and handsome volume is one of the few Syriac manuscripts in which extensive illustration is used in a highly developed style. The paintings appear to be by different hands, and while the relationship to Byzantine style can be seen, they are close in feeling and execution to the contemporary style of Islamic painting in Iraq. F.21 shows the Adoration of the Magi, the Christ child, with a nimbus, lies in swaddling clothes in the crib with ox and ass looking on, winged angels are above, and the three kings with haloes, to the left; at the bottom of the picture is a scene of the washing of the child. F.115a, Christ's entry into Jerusalem, is a scene depicted in an equally lively and charming manner, the bearded Christ with nimbus, and mounted on a donkey, is shown with ascetic features, in contrast to most of the disciples surrounding him; climbers in the trees break down the branches and birds fly above, while other onlookers peer out from a great house as the procession passes by.

30 **The Four Gospels.** Peshitta version with Greek vocalization, with Karshuni (Arabic translation in Syriac character), in parallel columns. This was copied by the priest Theodore in the village Akurta on Mount Lebanon, for the Archdeacon Abraham bar Theodore; with ornaments by the priest Kamar, from the village Deir Bali, 1437–38.

Add. 17983

The text is preceded by an ornamented table of lessons. The lessons are rubricated in the text. After the Islamic conquest, Arabic gradually supplanted Syriac in daily use; the Christian community adapted their Syriac script to the writing of Arabic by adding diacritics to represent sounds which did not occur in Syriac.

31 **Gospel Lectionary.** This is in the Peshitta version, and is arranged according to the Nestorian use. It was copied by Elia at Mosul in Iraq in 1499.

Add. 7174.

The Nestorians preferred the Peshitta to other Syriac versions of the scriptures throughout the centuries. This volume is illustrated: at ff.21b–22 is shown a scene of the Baptism of Christ, facing a floral carpet page in Persian style.

32 **Kitāb Manārat Al-Aḳdās.** This is a Karshuni manuscript, that is Arabic in Syriac script, translated from the Syriac, and copied on paper in 1696.

Or. 4410.

The original Syriac is entitled Menārath Ḳudhshē, or 'Lamp of the Sanctuary' by Gregory Bar-Hebraeus, (1226–86), the last and one of the greatest writers in Syriac. It is a treatise on the principles upon which the Church is founded, and so deals with natural and divine philosophy. At ff.5b–6 there is a diagram of the Tabernacle, and facing it an illuminated cross in a border

with branches containing words of a creed, resembling a candelabrum – an allusion to the title.

33 **Bazaar of Heraclides.** Teghurta dhe Herakledhos, by Nestorius, Patriarch of Constantinople. Copied in the Nestorian hand in 1906.

Or. 9046.

This respresents the final expression of the faith of Nestorius, after his condemnation at the Council of Ephesus in 431. In it he explains his view of the position of the blessed Virgin Mary, and of the nature of Christ. It remains one of the key texts relating to Nestorian theology.

34 **Nestorian Stone of Sianfu,** AD 781. This is a black limestone slab with a boldly carved crown, an inscription in Chinese prose and verse of approximately 2,000 characters, and at the base and sides, shorter portions in Syriac in the Estrangela character set on its side.
Rubbings in the British Library, 15406.a.6, 11, and 35.

(Plate 6)

According to the inscription, Christianity was brought to China about 635 by Alopen, who braved difficulties and dangers to bring sacred books from Syria. In 638, the Tang Emperor Tai-tsung issued a decree: 'Alopen, a Persian monk, having brought the religion of the Scriptures from afar, has come to offer it at the capital . . . Let the ministers build a monastery in the Iningfang [a city square in Sianfu] and let twenty-one men be admitted as monks'. After relating how Alopen became a Guardian of the Empire and Lord of the Great Law, an account of the progress of the Church down to 781, in the reign of the Emperor Tih-tsung is given. The Syriac portions are at the foot of the stone and on the sides, the latter containing names of monks given in Chinese and Syriac.

35 **A Nestorian Priest.** Chinese painting on silk. British Museum, Department of Oriental Antiquities. 1919 1–1 048

This head and shoulders painting of a Christian priest is reminiscent of Tang paintings of the Boddhisattva, but here crosses are to be seen in the costume of the subject, who also bears a staff.

36 The Gospel of St Matthew. Mongolian, Kalmuk. Moscow, 1815.

British and Foreign Bible Society.

The Mongol script, based on the Uighur of the fourteenth century, goes back to an adaptation of the Syriac, brought by the Nestorian missionaires and turned on its side, so that it was read from top to bottom. This was called *kalika*, and was adopted by the Kalmuks in 1648. Scripture translation in modern times was begun by the Russian Bible Society, and this version of St Matthew by Dr I. J. Schmidt was completed in 1809, and was the first portion to be printed in the Mongol language.

37 The Four Gospels. Arabic. Copied in Palestine, 1337: with portraits of the Evangelists and ornamented pages.

Add. 11856.

As Arabic became the dominant language of the Near East, it slowly supplanted Syriac, and in Egypt Coptic, and Christians adopted Arabic first in their daily lives, and then in the production of a Christian literature in that language. In the eighth century, an Arabic translation of the Psalms was made from the Peshitta version, but it was not till the thirteenth century that a systematic and official programme of the translation of the scriptures into Arabic was embarked upon.

38 Psalms. Arabic. Paper codex, copied in Egypt in the sixteenth century, in a Naskhi hand with Coptic glosses.

Arundel Oriental MS.15. (Plate 21)

This manuscript, written in a beautiful hand, has gold and blue floral verse dividers, occasional variants noted in red, and chapter headings in gold and blue. Like contemporary Islamic manuscripts it has an intricate geometric carpet page as a frontispiece.

39 Horologium. Services for the Canonical Hours, Latin and Arabic. Fano, 1514.

Or.70.aa.11

This is the earliest Arabic printed book. It contains a dedication to Pope Leo X.

40 Psalms. Multilingual version including Latin, Italian, Hebrew and Arabic. Genoa, 1516.

Or.70.d.8.

41 The Four Gospels. Arabic. Rome, De Proapaganda Fide, 1590–91.

Or.70.d.6. (Plate 24)

These are the earliest printed Arabic Gospels, and contain a series of woodcuts by A. Tempesta, many based on those of Albrecht Dürer's *Kleine Passion*. Through the dissemination of this volume in the Middle East, it influenced manuscript painting in Egypt and Ethiopia. Compare the illustration of Christ's healing two blind men (St Matthew 20.vv.30–34) at p.75, with the corresponding picture in the Ethiopic manuscript Or.510, f.51a (No. 65, below). See also No. 49, below.

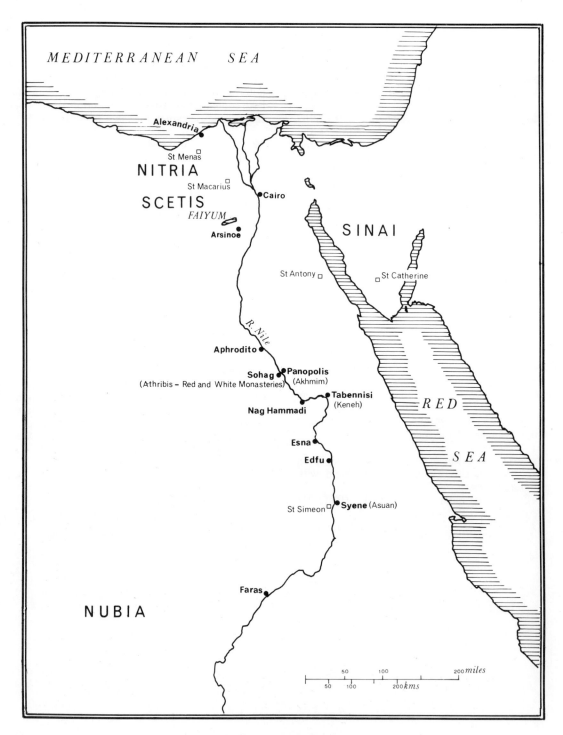

MEDITERRANEAN SEA

Alexandria

St Menas

NITRIA

St Macarius

SCETIS

Cairo

FAIYUM

Arsinoë

SINAI

St Antony

St Catherine

R. Nile

Aphrodito

Sohag

Panopolis
(Akhmim)

(Athribis – Red and White Monasteries)

Tabennisi
(Keneh)

Nag Hammadi

RED

Esna

SEA

Edfu

St Simeon

Syene (Asuan)

Faras

NUBIA

50   100   200 miles

50   100   200 kms

3 Christianity in Egypt

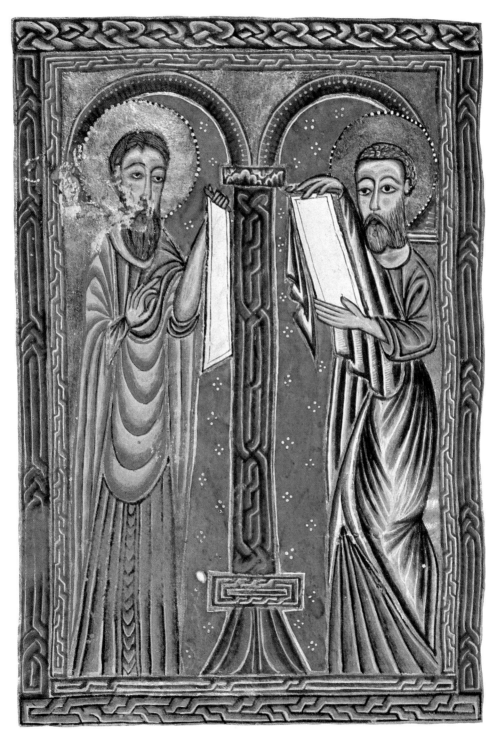

St Peter and St Paul. New Testament. Armenian, AD *1280.*
  Add.18549, f.161b. (Cat. No. 114)

St George and the Dragon. Four Gospels. Ethiopic. Seventeenth century.
  Or.516, f.99b. (Cat. No. 66)

4

The Church in Egypt and Nubia

The city of Alexandria, founded by Alexander the Great in 332 BC, displaced Athens as the greatest centre of art, learning and science of the ancient world. Under the Ptolemaic dynasty, Greek culture, dominated by Platonic philosophy, was combined with Egyptian and Jewish elements. In the third century BC, the Old Testament was translated into Greek, in the version known as the Septuagint, and was thence spread throughout the eastern Mediterranean region.

In 30 BC, Egypt was conquered by Octavian, later to be the Emperor Augustus, and remained a Roman province until the coming of the Arabs in AD 641. At the beginning of the Roman period, Philo, the Jewish scholar, following the Hellenistic tradition of Alexandria, developed the allegorical interpretation of scripture, enabling him to reconcile Greek philosophy with Hebrew religion and formulated a doctrine of the Logos, as the creative power which emenates from God, and by which man comes to know him.

The Gospel of St Matthew relates how after the visit of the Wise Men, Herod ordered the slaughter of the children of Bethlehem, but Joseph took Mary and the infant Jesus to Egypt, and only returned after Herod was dead. The apocryphal Gospel of Thomas suggests that Jesus was seven years old when the Holy Family left Egypt while a passage in the Talmud alleges that Jesus learnt his wonder-working powers while resident there.

The establishment of the Christian Church in Egypt is associated with St Mark the Evangelist, who was said to have been martyred in Alexandria in AD 63. His successor as first Bishop and Patriarch of Alexandria was Ananius, and thereafter the line has remained unbroken until the present day. The traditional Greek Eucharistic service of Alexandria was known as the Liturgy of St Mark, and when in later times the Coptic Church used its own language, it was a modified form of this rite which became standard as the Coptic Liturgy of St Mark.

The early persecutions which affected the Church in Egypt included those under the Emperor Trajan (98–117), Septimius Severus (in 202) and Decius (in 250). The worst sufferings of the Egyptian Christians, however, occurred under Diocletian, and the Copts still commemorate this fact by dating their documents by the *Era of Martyrs,* commencing from the first day of the Egyptian year in which that Emperor succeded, i.e. 29 August 284. The most famous martyr under Diocletian's persecution of 304 was St Menas, born to the south-west of Lake Mereotis, near Alexandria. His hometown became a centre of pilgrimage, associated with miraculous cures by water, and ampullae, or clay bottles with a figure of St Menas between camels became popular. He was the patron saint of merchants.

THE CATECHETICAL SCHOOL OF ALEXANDRIA

In the second century AD, doctrinal speculation became a prominent feature of Church life, which in its more extreme form expressed itself in the heretical Gnostic movement. The Church's reaction to the Gnostics was to formulate its own position openly and clearly. This it did by determining the Canon of Scripture, by appealing to the authority of the Bishops as the guarantors of the authentic tradition, and by summarizing basic Christian doctrines in credal formulae. These developments partly account for the importance of the Catechetical School of Alexandria and the activities of the Patriarchs in making pronouncements on doctrine to the Christian world at large.

The first of the great teachers whose works have been preserved was Clement of Alexandria (*c.*150–215). He was an Athenian, and came to study under Pantaenus, and succeeded him as head of the School in 190, a position he held till 202, when he had to flee during the persecutions of Septimius Severus. Clement believed that Greek philosophy was a divine gift, and that Christ as Logos was both the source of all human reason and the interpreter of God to mankind. He considered ignorance and false belief as worse than sin and took an optimistic view of the ultimate destiny of even the most erring.

Clement was succeeded by Origen (185–254), who was only seventeen when Clement had fled in 202. Born in Egypt of Christian parents, Clement had studied at the Catechetical School, led an ascetic life, studied the pagan philosophers, and made journeys in search of knowledge to Rome and to Arabia. He worked as a layman and became famous as a biblical critic and interpreter of the scriptures and as a theologian and writer on spiritual matters. In 215 when troubles broke out in Alexandria during the visit of the Emperor Caracalla, he went to Palestine and taught there, but was recalled to Alexandria to continue his work. On a second visit to Palestine in 230 he was ordained priest against the wishes of the Patriarch of Alexandria, so he went into exile and founded the School at Caesarea, where he continued his teaching till the time of persecution under Decius about 250.

34

The third century saw the development of the ascetic life. This owes most to St Antony the Great (*c*.251–356). He was a Copt; not a scholar, but a contemplative. At the age of nineteen he was converted by hearing the story of the Rich Young Man from the Gospel. He gave up his wealth, and spent the next fifteen years in a hut near his home in ascetic practice. Then in 285 he retired to the desert, where he is said to have fought with demons under the guise of wild beasts. The holiness and discipline which he attained contrasted with the evils of the contemporary secular culture and compared favourably with the more extreme austerities practised by other solitary ascetics, and so he attracted numbers of disciples. About 305 he organized them into a community of hermits living under a rule. He was orthodox in his beliefs, and supported St Athanasius against the Arians.

A younger contemporary was St Pachomius (*c*.290–346), the founder of coenobitic monasticism – organized communities living together under rule. He was born in Upper Egypt and, released after army service, was converted to Christianity and baptized. For three years he was a disciple of the hermit Palaemon, then in 320 he built a monastery at Tabennisi on the east bank of the Nile, and by his holiness attracted a large number of monks to join him. By the time of his death, there were nine monasteries for men, and two for women.

St Macarius (*c*.300–390) was another native of Upper Egypt, who at the age of thirty joined a colony of monks in the Desert of Scete and became renowned for his sanctity and miracles. A little to the north, in the Nitrian Desert, west of the mouths of the Nile, a famous centre of hermit life grew up under St Ammon in the mid-fourth century. One of the renowned monasteries here, that of the Syrians, St Mary Deipara, was a major source of the great collections of Syriac manuscripts now in the Vatican and in the British Library.

AN AGE OF CONTROVERSY

In the fourth century some of the most serious controversies arose to trouble the Church. Arius (*c*.250–336), a Libyan, became a priest of one of the principal churches of Alexandria. He was ascetic in manner and an able preacher, but his doctrine of God made it appear that the Trinity was really three Gods, with Christ in an inferior position. The Patriarch condemned this teaching in 318, but still it spread. At the Council of Nicea in 325 the teaching of Arius was condemned, largely through the influence of St Athanasius (295–373), who in 328 himself succeeded to the See of Alexandria. His writings include a famous treatise on the Incarnation, and defences of orthodoxy against the Arian teaching. He was also a friend of the monks, including Antony and Pachomius, and wrote a biography of St Antony.

Meanwhile, further controversies disturbed the Church and these tended to reinforce, or be reinforced by, the rivalries between Alexandria and Constantinople, the new capital of the Eastern Roman Empire. This was brought to a head by St Cyril, Bishop of Alexandria from 412 to 444. He was a theologian of the greatest ability, but forthright and determined in ecclesiastical politics. He entered into many disputes in defence of the faith, but especially with Nestorius. Cyril drew up his position in a letter which was approved by the Council of Ephesus in 431 and ratified by the Council of Chalcedon in 451, after his death. He was by nature domineering and impatient and his character contributed to the growing rift between Alexandria and Constantinople.

The break came in the patriarchate of his successor, Dioscorus, who soon after his accession in 444 adopted the Monophysite teaching that in the person of Christ there was but a single, divine nature. This teaching was condemned at Chalcedon in 451 and he was deposed and exiled. This led to a split in the Church in Egypt, which has never since been healed. The followers of the Byzantine Emperor Marcianus at Chalcedon, who maintained the Trinitarian faith, were henceforward represented by a minority in Egypt, known as the Melkite or Royalist church and had some 300,000 followers, many of them in government positions. For the rest of the Egyptian population, Monophysitism represented their national cult and their opposition to Byzantium and received support from the monks.

This was the period when a more distinctively Egyptian Church developed, using Coptic rather than Greek as its medium, reflecting the dominance of the popular, national element, rather than the cosmopolitan outlook of earlier times. This trend is represented by the Abbot Shenute (died *c.* 450) of the White Monastery at Athribis, west of Sohag on the Upper Nile, where he became the Superior in 388. His community greatly increased – there were 2,200 monks and 1,800 nuns. His rule was severe and he introduced flogging for minor faults and written professions of obedience from the monks. He accompanied St Cyril to Ephesus in 431 and shared a like harshness of temperament. The White Monastery became an important centre of literary activity in the Sahidic or Southern dialect of Coptic and an important part of the British Library's collection of Coptic manuscripts is from this source.

Rivalry with Constantinople continued, but the Council of the Church held in that city in 553 made some concessions to the Egyptian point of view. However, the Persians invaded Egypt in 616 and held the country till they were expelled by the Emperor Heraclius in 629.

THE RISE OF ISLAM

In the meanwhile, Islam had come into being in Arabia, founded by the prophet Muhammad (*c.* 570–629). In 638 a Muslim army headed by 'Amr ibn 'Asi came

36

down from Syria and invaded Egypt, with the connivance of the Coptic Christians who preferred them to the hated Byzantines. At first the Arabs respected the Christian community, but from 704 the Arabs began severe persecutions against the Copts during the patriarchate of Bishop Alexander (704–722). He had twice to pay 6000 dinars, and a tax on every monk. The Copts were next stripped of their possessions and every monk received a brand on his hand, with his name, number and the name of his monastery; every monk without the mark had his hand cut off. Crosses and pictures were destroyed, images broken and churches pulled down.

The position of the Christians deteriorated. Because of the intelligence and usefulness of the Copts many of them were employed in official positions, but there was intrigue and sporadic violence in the relations between the two communities under the Caliph Al-Hakim (996–1021), and at the beginning of the Bahri Mamluk dynasty during the patriarchate of Bishop Athanasius (1251–60). From then onwards till 1882, the Coptic Church suffered increasing weakness and poverty, till after the battle of Tel el-Kebir, they received guaranteed freedom of worship once again.

CHURCH LIFE

The externals of Coptic Church life have much in common with that of other Eastern and Orthodox Churches, including such features as the architecture and decoration of Church buildings, the vestments and the forms of liturgy. Their most distinctive doctrine is that concerning the nature of Christ, in which they differ from the teaching of the Western and Greek Orthodox Churches.

The customs of the Copts, however, have some special characteristics, some of which have come down from ancient days in Egypt, and others show Islamic influence. The Copts are baptized as children and they believe that it is at that time they are endowed with the Holy Spirit. They practice circumcision, in common not only with the Muslims but also their own ancestors. Boys are taught the Psalms, the Gospels and Epistles in Arabic, and the Gospels and Epistles in Coptic also. Prayers are said seven times a day: at dawn, 9.0 a.m., midday, 3.0 p.m., 5.0 p.m., 6.0 p.m. and midnight. The Copts pray facing the east. The Eucharist is celebrated at daybreak and lasts for three hours. They make their confession before going to Communion. In their liturgies, they say that God was crucified, reflecting their monophysite teaching. They have no images, but use pictures of their saints.

The Copts are said to constitute about six per cent of the modern Egyptian population, or about 3,000,000 people. The head of their Church is the Patriarch of Alexandria, but he now resides in Cairo, and is always chosen from among the monks of the Monastery of St Antony, near the Red Sea.

Coptic is the language of the Egyptians as it was spoken by the inhabitants of the Nile valley and delta during the Christian era. By the end of the second century, its speakers had successively discarded the hieroglyphic, hieratic and demotic scripts and had begun to use the archaic Greek alphabet, with seven additional characters adapted from demotic for sounds not found in Greek. Its two main dialects are Sahidic and Bohairic. The former was the chief literary dialect from the time of the emergence of Coptic writing in the third century until it was gradually superseded by Bohairic during the eleventh-twelfth century.

After the coming of Islam, the Copts became bilingual and finally Arabic-speaking, retaining their old language and script only for Bibles and service books and even these were eventually accompanied by Arabic translations, rubrics and colophons, not to mention Islamic ornamentation. Bohairic is still in use today for religious purposes.

COPTIC LITERATURE

The Coptic literature that has come down to us is almost entirely religious. Even the laws and history are really canon law and church history. Apart from translations of biblical books, the oldest known Coptic works were written by the Gnostics, proponents of a mysterious, esoteric anti-religion of inverse monotheism which latched on to Christianity and Judaism in such a way as to entrap undiscerning believers into thinking it was part of them. Alarmed at this threat, the Church Fathers as well as the early Rabbis stamped it out as a dangerous heresy and their books were condemned to destruction. Little was known of them, and that mostly from the works of their opponents, until the discovery in 1946 of a whole Coptic Gnostic library of the fourth century in a desert wadi in southern Egypt.

Between the Roman persecutions of Christians and the Byzantine hounding of 'schismatics', the Copts enjoyed a couple of centuries of peace during which some of their finest writers flourished. They produced liturgies, homilies, canons of church law and monastic regulations, lives of saints and martyrs, theological treatises. The early period brought forth some chroniclers and historians and some fiction. It was only as the spoken language declined that Coptic grammars and dictionaries were compiled – in Arabic – in the eleventh century. The thirteenth century saw almost the last glimmer of Coptic literary creation and since then Copts have made their contribution to Arabic literature.

Coptic literature is almost wholly derivative and the volumes in the British Library collection are representative of its range and importance. The bulk of it, coming as it does from monastic libraries, is Christian in content: Biblical texts, apocrypha, the lives of saints and martyrs, homiletic works. The earlier Biblical texts, like that of

Deuteronomy, Jonah and Acts (No.42) are important for the study of the transmission of the Greek text of the Bible, of which the Coptic is a translation. Among Bohairic texts, which for the most part are late in date, liturgical books predominate.

MANUSCRIPTS

The older Coptic MSS (to about the ninth century) are mostly on papyrus. Few of these were well preserved when found; indeed, some of our greatest treasures were literally dug out of the rubbish heaps of ancient villages or rescued from the fuel piles of defunct monasteries whose inhabitants no longer understood the texts. These papyrus MSS are rarely coloured and such drawings or patterns as they contain are generally on the first and last pages and around the margins – the first parts to suffer damage and destruction – so there is little of visual interest here. A Coptic papyrus amulet of the third century is included with the Ethiopic collection for comparison (see No.89, below).

Some very old parchment codices have survived better and we have one or two quite venerable illuminated ones. Later, paper comes into use alongside parchment and coloured decoration becomes more common: elaborate geometric and interlaced patterns in frontispiece crosses, headpieces, borders and panels; enlarged and sometimes coloured capitals at the beginnings of paragraphs and – almost exclusively Coptic – marginal scrolls in the shape of birds (possibly the direct descendants of the hieroglyphics). Gold is absent – at least in British Library MSS – until the late eighteenth century, perhaps because the Copts with all their persecutions and oppressions could not afford it. Yellow paint seems to take its place. Red ink or paint is also used boldly with striking effect. Green has often faded to a dull brown and blue is less common.

Coptic leather bindings are the oldest known, and influenced development both in the Islamic world and in Europe (see Appendix, items 140–49, below).

42 Deuteronomy, Jonah and Acts. A papyrus codex in the Sahidic dialect in uncials, of the early fourth century

Or.7594 (Plate 1)

This volume contains some of the earliest known Coptic versions of Biblical texts. The titles are given at the ends of the books. After Acts, there follows an apocryphal work of Jewish-Christian inspiration, 'The Apocalypse of Elias', written in a semi-cursive hand.

43 Didache. A fragment on fine papyrus of a Sahidic version of the Didache, of the fifth century.

Or.9271.

The Didache, 'teaching, doctrine', is an early Christian manual on morals and Church practice, whose authorship and exact date are unknown. The complete text contains sixteen chapters on ethics, on the sacraments, prayer and church orders, and is of special interest for its evidence on the development of the liturgy. It was originally composed in Greek, perhaps in Syria.

44 The Martyrdom of St Mercurius. Sahidic manuscript on parchment, copied in 985. From Edfu in Upper Egypt.

Or.6801.

The beginning of the manuscript has a miniature of a miracle of St Mercurius: the saint, mounted on horseback, is spearing a man whose donkey is looking round at him in disdain or reproach, for the man had desecrated the church dedicated to St Mercurius. The latter rode out of his picture and transfixed the offender, who promised to become a Christian if released.

45 Encomium of St Michael, the Archangel. Coptic (Sahidic), on parchment, dated 987. From Edfu in Upper Egypt.

Or.7021.

This hymn of praise was composed by Theodosius, Patriarch of Alexandria in the sixth century. At f.1a it contains a portrait of the Archangel Michael in the vestments of a Coptic priest. The painting is unfinished.

46 A Book of Homilies. This is in the Sahidic dialect, a parchment codex, copied by Philotheos the Deacon at Ḥrit in the Faiyum, partly dated 989–990.

Or.6782.

This manuscript contains a collection of hagiographical texts, of which the first is an apocryphal work, entitled 'The Repose of St John, the Evangelist and Apostle of Christ'. The work contains miniatures, including at f.1b St John, with the Virgin Mary suckling her child (who is holding a book instead of the breast), and on the opposite page an elaborate decorated heading, with birds at the beginning of the text.

47 Four Gospels. Coptic and Arabic, with the Evangelists pictured and illuminations in the text, copied in 1173.

Bodleian Library, Oxford. Hunt 17. (Plate 9)

The volume opens with a large coloured cross, with at the bottom, left, St Matthew seated, writing, and to the right Jesus, with halo, giving a blessing. The opposite page has an extensive and elaborate heading with the beginning of the Coptic text of the Gospel, and the Arabic in a narrow column on the right.

48 Orders of a Deacon. This is a paper document in the Bohairic dialect of Coptic, and Arabic, from Akhmim, 1363.

Or.5464 (Plate 20)

Philotheos, Bishop of Panopolis (Akhmim), in Upper Egypt, makes Gabriel, son of Michael, a full deacon in the church of St Theodore the General, to the west of Christians' Square, on the 17th of the month Pachon in the Year of the Martyrs 1079 (=1363). The muddy brown ink must originally have been gold or bright green. The text is ornamented with a cross and birds.

49 The Four Gospels. Coptic (Bohairic) and Arabic, copied on paper in 1663.

Or.1316. (Plate 27)

This volume was dedicated by John, the 105th Patriarch of Alexandria in the Church of the Virgin and St George in Cairo, in 1731. It contains a number of miniatures of Gospel scenes, some with European antecedents in their style, apparently going back to Tempesta's woodcuts in the Arabic Gospels printed in Rome in 1591 (see No. 41, above). This volume is also notable for its fine cover.

50 The Four Gospels. Coptic (Bohairic) and Arabic, copied in the early eighteenth century.

Or.1317.

This volume has the Eusebian sections and Canons, a decorative cross, a series of miniatures of Gospel scenes, and a fine binding. It contains the signature of Peter, 109th Patriarch of Alexandria, 1815, to whom the book belonged.

The permanent exhibition in the Coptic Corridor, near the Fourth Egyptian Room of the British Museum includes a wide range of objects from Roman and Christian Egypt, which demonstrate how both Egyptian and classical customs and artistic traditions contributed to the formation of Coptic art where the themes and symbolism were wholly Christian. Masonry fragments from Coptic churches include acanthus friezes, and highly decorated capitals with vine-leaf designs. Coptic textiles, mostly fragmentary, show how hellenized concepts were gradually transformed for the representation of Christian themes, while stylistically they became less naturalistic, and more decorative, angular and formalized, even heraldic in idiom. Coptic figure carving on tombstones tended to chunky formal frontalization, disregarding anatomical proportions, but not without power in the facial expressions, and where the normally used colour has survived, the whole effect is of some charm. Objects in metal, wood and pottery for use in church or home, or by pilgrims, are frequently decorated with crosses and other religious themes. A selection of these objects are described in association with manuscripts to show the development and continuity of Coptic art.

The following items are from the British Museum collections, Department of Egyptian Antiquities (EA), and Department of Medieval and Later Antiquities (MLA).

51 **Textile Fragment.** From Akhmim, Upper Egypt, eighth century.

EA 65662.

On a red background, two biblical scenes are shown in roundels: David and Saul, and David with his harp.

52 **Linen Tunic,** with applied tapestry ornament. From Egypt, eighth century. MLA 1901/3-11/1, (on loan to the Department of Egyptian Antiquities). Gift of the executors of Major W. J. Myers, 1901.

The vertical stripes on the tunic depict the Virgin and Child, and the roundels on the lower part of the tunic show the Adoration of the Magi.

53 **Bronze Cross,** with roundel depicting St Peter at the centre.

EA 59741.

54 **Clay Lamp,** with a prayer to Bishop Joseph. From Akhmim.

EA 23330.

55 **Pilgrim Bottle.** Clay, with a figure of St Menas between two camels. From Egypt.

MLA EC 860.

56 **Pilgrim Bottle.** Clay, with inscription eulogizing St Menas. From Egypt.

MLA EC 964.

57 **Pilgrim Bottle.** Clay. From Egypt.

EA 23327.

58 **Jar Sealing,** with Christian Chi-Rho symbol. From Egypt, fifth-sixth centuries.

EA 67791.

59 **Coptic Tombstone,** of the monk Victor. Sandstone. From Saqqara, the Monastery of Apa Jeremias, sixth-eighth centuries.

EA 1525.

The head has a triangular form, enclosing an arch, with the Coptic inscription below, then a cross in a roundel, and a bird with spread wings at the base.

60 A Saint on Horseback. Limestone relief. From Egypt.

EA 1216.

Figures of horsemen appear frequently in Coptic art, including textiles and miniature painting, and this theme was frequently applied to the depiction of Christian saints, as in the examples of St Menas (Cat.No.61a), and St Mercurius, (Cat.No.44).

NUBIA

The lands of the Nile above the First Cataract at Aswan constituted the ancient region of Nubia, and included the Nobadae, the Makorite kingdom further south, and the Alodae on the lower reaches of the Blue Nile. As these lands had long been influenced by Egypt, there were probably some Christians there from early times; but the first systematic attempt to convert the people was in the reign of the Roman Emperor Justinian, in the middle of the sixth century. His wife, Theodora, supported the Monophysites, and a Coptic priest, Julian, was sent from Alexandria on a mission to the Nobadae. Soon afterwards, Justinian sent Orthodox missionaires, and being forestalled among the Nobadae, they went on to the Makorites and converted the people there.

Christian kingdoms with links with the Coptic Church continued for many centuries, even after the rise of the Islamic empire, up to about the fourteenth century, and there are many sites along the upper Nile valley where there are Christian remains, including tombstones with Greek and Coptic inscriptions. The island of Philae, near Aswan, long a centre of worship of Isis and Osiris, in Justinian's time was made a bishopric, and provided a link between the Churches in Egypt and Nubia.

Faras, the ancient Pachoras, twenty miles north of Wadi Halfa, was the capital of Nubia till the eighth century. Since the construction of the new Aswan Dam in 1962, the site has been under water, but archaeological and conservation work sponsored by UNESCO, with the major participation of the Poles, established the cathedral site, and resulted in the rescue of frescoes dating from the eighth to the twelfth centuries.

Early in the eighth century, King Mercurius, having united the Nubian kingdoms, transferred his capital to Dongola, between the Third and Fourth Cataracts.

The British Library possesses one of the few surviving books in a Nubian dialect: this is a small manuscript containing two texts:

61a A Miracle of St Menas; and a Sermon on The Canons of Nicea. Nubian text, copied in 1053.

Or.6805 (Plate 7)

Ff,9b-10a include the end of the story about St Menas, and an outline figure illustrating its climax, showing the saint on horseback, who had come down from an ikon in his church at Alexandria, to cure a woman of her barrenness who had appealed to him.

61b Texts relating to Saint Mena of Egypt and Canons of Nicea. In a Nubian dialect. With facsimile. Edited by E. A. Wallis Budge. Trustees of the British Museum: London, 1909. (Plate of f.1b of Or.6805).

14005.1.1

62 Items from the Grave of Bishop Timotheus. From Qasr Ibrim. British Museum, Department of Medieval and Later Antiquities, 1971/8–1/1–6.
(a) Wooden Pectoral, with carving of an angel, twelfth-thirteenth century.
(b) Wooden Cross, crudely carved.
(c) Iron Cross, perhaps part of a lamp suspension.
(d) Iron Cross, with trifoliate arms, and a stem with loop for suspension from the neck.
(e) Pottery Stamp, for Eucharistic bread, with Greek inscription *Michael* on one side, and on the flat side small crosses for marking the bread.
(f) Linen Mappa, with blue border.

Bishop Timotheus was enthroned on the 19th of the month Hathor in the Year of the Martyrs 1088 (AD 1371–2). *See*: J. M. Plumley: *The Scrolls of Bishop Timotheus*. London, 1975.

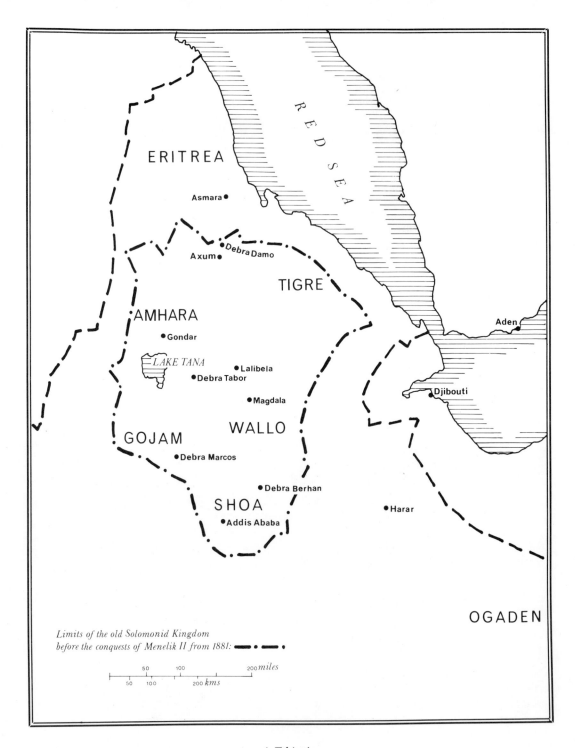

ERITREA

Asmara ●

R E D   S E A

Axum ● ●Debra Damo

TIGRE

Aden ●

AMHARA

Gondar ●

LAKE TANA

●Lalibela

●Debra Tabor

●Magdala

Djibouti ●

WALLO

GOJAM

●Debra Marcos

●Debra Berhan

SHOA

●Addis Ababa

● Harar

OGADEN

Limits of the old Solomonid Kingdom
before the conquests of Menelik II from 1881: ▬ ▪ ▬ ▪

50   100   200 *miles*
─────────────────────────────
50   100   200 *kms*

4 *Ethiopia*

5

The Church in Ethiopia

ETHIOPIA AND ITS HISTORY

A hellenized pagan dynasty existed in Axum, in the northern Tigre province as early as the second century AD. In the reign of King Ezana, a Tyrian missionary, St Frumentius, arrived about 330 and state recognition to Christianity was given. Frumentius was consecrated bishop by St Athanasius, patriarch of Alexandria, and returned to Ethiopia.

At the end of the fifth century, nine 'Roman', i.e. Byzantine missionaries came, probably from Syria, but it is not certain whether they were Monophysites or Chalcedonians. A cathedral was built at Axum. The outstanding event in the history of Axum was the invasion of Southern Arabia by the Emperor Caleb, at the behest of the Byzantine Emperor Justin I (518–527), to overthrow the Jewish ruler of Himyar, 523–525, but he was not able to hold his position there very long. Yared, an Abuna of this period, composed the Degua (hymnal). When c.640 the Patriarchate of Alexandria was transferred to Cairo, the Ethiopic Church was made dependent on it and its Monophysite incumbent. In the next centuries, there was trouble from Muslim and Jewish groups. In the tenth century, a Jewish princess, Juditta, destroyed Axum.

A new Christian dynasty, the Zagwe, of the Agao tribe of Lasta, south of Axum, ruled from 1137 to 1268. The most famous of this line was King Lalibala of Lasta (1190–1225). He was responsible for the construction of the nine rock-cut churches at Lalibela.

In 1270 the old 'Solomonic' dynasty was restored by Yekuno Amlak, who ousted the last Zagwe ruler and ruled from 1270 to 1285. At the same time, church reform was undertaken by the energetic Abuna or Archbishop, Takla Haymanot. He supported the monarchy and a new national spirit emerged. Later he retired from active affairs and became an extreme ascetic, living in a spiked cell, in a standing position. He is a favourite saint of the Ethiopic Church.

Yekuno Amlak's grandson, Amda Sion I (1314–44) consolidated the power of the kingdom and in his time, the epic *Kebra Nagast* was composed, which included the traditional story of the foundation of the Ethiopic monarchy through the union of King Solomon with the Queen of Sheba. In this reign, chronicles and law books were also compiled. The greatest ruler of this dynasty was Zara Ya'qob (1434–68). He introduced military and religious reforms and encouraged literature. This was the period when the Miracles of the Virgin Mary became popular, originally being adapted from an Arabic version.

Lebna Dengel (1508–40) struggled against the Muslims. His successor, Claudis (1540–59) defeated the Grañ (Ahmad ibn Ibrahim) in 1542 and so stayed the Muslim advance.

Gondar was the Ethiopic capital from the sixteenth to eighteenth centuries. King Fasildas (1632–67) submitted to the Church of Rome but later repudiated this and resumed the connection between Church and State.

The rise of Kassa to become the Emperor Theodore III, saw Ethiopia coming out of its long isolation. The capital was transferred to Magdala. Misunderstandings with Britain led to the invasion under Sir Robert Napier, the capture of Magdala in 1868 and Theodore's suicide. In 1928, Ras Tafari became king and in 1930 ruled as the Emperor Haile Selassie until 1975.

ETHIOPIC LANGUAGE AND SCRIPT

Ethiopic is a Semitic language basically not very different from Arabic, and its script is almost the same as the characters found on South Arabian inscriptions, but turned on their sides. In two respects, however, Ethiopic script is unique in the Semitic family: it is written from left to right (perhaps an indication that this script was introduced with Christianity, by Greeks); and it is not purely consonantal, but shows vowel sounds by attaching various dashes and loops to one corner or another of the letters, so becoming not an alphabet, but a syllabary (rather like Sanskrit) of 287 characters including numerals and Amharic modifications.

Classical Ethiopic – or Ge'ez as its speakers called it – was spoken at Axum in northern Ethiopia. No one knows how long ago it became the dominant language of the Ethiopian empire – inscriptions date back to the third or fourth century; nor can anyone tell when it ceased to be used in daily speech, but by the time of its great flowering as a literary language, in the thirteenth–fourteenth centuries, it had already given way in speech to Amharic, the current official language of the country and one of the few among Ethiopia's eighty-odd vernaculars to have produced a written literature.

Amharic is basically Semitic but thickly overlaid with African vocabulary and constructions. It is written in the Ge'ez script with modifications. Ge'ez, like Syriac and Coptic, and like Latin in the Roman Catholic world, survives as a Church language.

46

Ethiopic as a written language is, apart from inscriptions on coins and obelisks, younger than the others. It was about 490 that nine Syrian missionaries arrived in Axum and started to translate the Bible and prayers for the people who may have embraced Christianity 150 years before. The Ethiopic Bible – which numbers 84 books in its canon – has preserved some apocryphal books no longer known in the original Greek, Coptic or Syriac and the fourteen Ethiopian liturgies likewise include some which are lost in their original languages.

The Arabs did not advance up the Nile further than Nubia, but their conquest of Egypt had the effect of isolating Ethiopia from the rest of Christendom for 600 years or more, except for the occasional traveller who brought back tales of the wonderful kingdom of Prester John. During this dark age, Ge'ez picked up lives of saints and martyrs, both translations from Arabic (from Coptic originals) and of native origin; canons of civil and church law; and cycles of legends such as the Alexander stories current throughout the Middle East. The real flowering of the language as a literary medium came with the spurt of national consciousness after 1270 when King Yekuno Amlak, claiming descent from the ancient kings of Axum who traced their line to Solomon and the Queen of Sheba, ousted the last of the Zagwe kings and established the dynasty which reigned until 1975. The event was celebrated by the composition (purporting to be a translation from Arabic) of *Kebra Nagast*, or the Glory of the Kings, the national epic of the country, tracing its history from Adam to Solomon and thence from the Queen of Sheba down to its own time.

There were other chronicles, collections of laws, folklore, medicine, and of natural sciences. Like the Copts, the Ethiopians appear to have shown a preference for the violence of apocalyptic and martyrology, while they have taken over the Coptic stress on mariolatry and carried it even further, as reflected in the popularity of the Miracles of the Virgin, Prayers to the Virgin, and so on. These Marian tales and prayers were compiled in the fifteenth century.

Islam had, however, made inroads from another direction – across the Red Sea. Vandalous Turkish invaders during the 1530s brought matters to a head. The desperate Negus brought in the Portuguese who were at the height of their explorations and global expansion, and with whose aid the Muslims were contained once and for all. A mere six years of ravage had seen the wholesale destruction of churches and monasteries with their occupants and their contents. The work of reconstruction saw a new outburst of literary fruitfulness – still in Ge'ez, notwithstanding that it was little used in current speech by then. Amharic manuscripts are rarely found before the eighteenth century. These are usually secular in character and not really literary (letters, records, etc.) except for some folk tales, until this century.

The Ethiopians really went all out to beautify their MSS. They made use of decorative borders and headbands and also of plaited bands between chapters, while red ink is noticeable on nearly every page, often being used for the first two lines of every chapter or page and for picking out the names of saints, angels, Mary or Jesus – or the owner or donor of a book. But the real distinction of the Ethiopic MSS is in the profusion of miniatures. The Syrians and Copts may have been handicapped by poverty or inhibited by the Islamic aversion to images, or the Ethiopians may have inherited something Egyptian or pan-African. Much has been said and written about Byzantine influence, Italian influence, Indian influence, the influence of the Arabic Gospels printed in Rome in 1590 (with engravings inspired by Dürer's prints), but in the end it is easy to see what is characteristically Ethiopian about the miniatures of all periods and all styles: naiveté; boldness of colour – nearly all of it bright reds, blues, yellows and greens; a certain serenity of expression, even in animals; dramatic vividness of action. Even when only red and black are used, striking effects are achieved.

The typical binding for Ethiopic manuscripts is of boards, often lined with cloth, and then at a later date covered with tooled brown leather. (See Appendix, nos 152–6).

An interesting class of Ethiopian materials is the protective amulets, used against sickness, or in time of war. A selection, with some Coptic and Syriac examples for comparison is described at Nos. 89–103.

63 The Octateuch. Vellum manuscript, written in a large, elegant character of the fifteenth century.
Or.480.

This volume contains the first eight books of the Old Testament, and is one of the few in the British Library collection of the period prior to the Muslim invasions of Ethiopia. The beginning of each book, except Ruth, is decorated with an intertwined design in red and black, called *harag*. The Ethiopian script, a syllabary of over 200 characters is shown here to great advantage; the use of alternative red and black lines of writing is purely for effect.

64 Octateuch, Gospels and Ecclesiastical Works. This is a vellum manuscript written in a small elegant character of the late seventeenth century, profusely decorated with coloured borders and devices, and with many illustrations.
Or.481.

This volume has, besides the first eight books of the Old Testament and the Four Gospels, numerous short works on church order, canons of Ecumenical Councils, and various discourses. The pictures include Moses, Aaron, Ruth; Eusebius and Carpianus, followed by decorated Canon Tables; incidents from the life of Christ, and portraits of the Evangelists. At f.99a is an attractive rendering of the 'Annunciation of Zacharias'. The Temple in Jerusalem is shown as if it were an Ethiopian church circular in plan, with a roof surmounted by a cross. Within, the haloed figures of the angel and Zacharias are both holding staves with crosses; ostriches on either side of the roof are reminiscent of the peacocks in earlier scenes of the fountain of life, as often represented in the Canon Tables.

65 The Four Gospels. Vellum manuscript, beautifully written in three columns in 1664–65, for King John I, 'A'lāf Sagad, and his queen, Sabla Wangēl, profusely illustrated.
Or.510. (Plate 25)

This manuscript is one which shows the use of European models for the illustrations. Hugo Buchthal demonstrated the dependence of the representation of Christ being nailed to the Cross, at f.117b as going back to a woodcut from Dürer's *Kleine Passion*; later it was shown that the borrowing came through the illustrations of A. Tempesta, based on Dürer, in the Arabic Gospels published in Rome in 1590–91. This relationship can be studied in another picture from the present manuscript, at f.51a of Christ healing two blind

men (Matthew 20, vv.30–34), and the corresponding Tempesta woodcut, both illustrated here. In the process of copying, the pictures were made Ethiopian: perspective was eliminated, and the presentation was simplified. This manuscript represents the classical first style of painting at Gondar. (Cf. No. 41, above).

66 The Four Gospels. Vellum, written by Mahanta Mikael in a good hand of the seventeenth century.
Or.516 (Coloured Plate IV)

This volume includes portraits of the Evangelists and their disciples, and there is a picture of St George slaying the dragon. The first page of each Gospel is also decorated. The style of these illustrations is different from most other Ethiopian painting, and only two or three other manuscripts have comparable examples, so it probably represents the personal idiom of the artist. The presentation is sternly linear and geometrical, and the predominence of reds, blacks and yellows is an archaising continuation of an older tradition. St Matthew is shown at f.4b with four acolytes; and St Mark at 64b. with two, while St Luke at f.100b has his attendants holding swords instead of the usual books, and there are two birds. St George is shown at f.99b with a yellow halo and a red chequered costume, seated on a small-headed white horse, spearing the dragon who has reeled onto his back under the horse's feet.

67 Four Gospels. Vellum manuscript, written in a good hand in 1675–6.
Or.515.

The volume includes the Epistle of Eusebius to Carpianus, the Eusebian Canons, introductory paragraphs and indexes to each Gospel, which is also prefaced by a portrait of the Evangelist with his symbol. That of St Luke shows him seated writing, while a winged heavenly ox holds his inkhorn.

68 The Revelation of St John. This is a vellum manuscript, written in a large elegant character, probably of the early eighteenth century.
Or.533.

This volume also includes the Acts of St John at Ephesus, attributed to his disciple Prochorus, the Death of John, narrated by Prochorus and a hymn of the scribe. Among the subjects illustrated are the Lamb in the midst of the Throne, worshipped by the four beasts and the four and twenty elders (Rev.5, vv.5–8, at ff.18b–19a); the seven angels of Rev.8 v.6, poised ready to sound, however, not trumpets but drums; and the angels sounding, followed by hail, fire and blood, and the destruction of the third part of the ships (Rev.8, vv.7–9, at ff.34b–35a.). This manuscript passed from an earlier owner, whose name has everywhere been erased, to King Iyasu, who acceded in 1730, and his queen Wolatta Giyorgis.

69 Mestira Zaman. A biblical History in verse, vol. 1. Written in a fine hand during the early part of the eighteenth century. The colophon, which has been much altered by erasure, gives the name of 'Īyāsū II, but that of Bakāfā appears on the same page, so that the volume was probably written between 1721 and 1730.

Or.790.

The full title is Gūbā'ē Mesṭīrāta Zamanāt, or 'Collections of the Mysteries of the Times'. The book contains many pictures, some of which are only partly finished, and others in outline only, which makes it possible to study the artist's technique. At ff.16b–17a a completed sequence shows incidents from the story of Joseph, including his dream of the sun, moon and stars; Jacob's sending him to his brothers; his being sold into slavery at the mouth of the pit; with, on the facing page, Joseph waiting on his master, Potiphar; then with Potiphar's wife; leaving his coat behind, and with the butler and baker in prison, with representations of their dreams.

70 Prayers to The Virgin Mary. Manuscript on vellum, copied in the fifteenth century.

Or.13156.

This small manuscript is the earliest illustrated one in the British Library's Ethiopic collection. It contains eight portraits of saints, including at ff.144a–145b, that of St Onuphrius, in the Byzantine pose of a standing figure holding a book, in a simple, medieval style. The facing page has an ornamental headband around the beginning of a prayer. (Cf. No. 149, below).

71 Miracles of the Blessed Virgin Mary. *Ta'āmra Māryām.* This vellum manuscript was written in a large and beautiful hand of the middle of the seventeenth century, the main portion being copied in the reign of Fāsīladas (1632–67). It contains numerous illustrations.

Or.641. (Plate 26)

The Miracles of Mary became a favourite devotional work of the Ethiopian Church. The collection began in France in the twelfth century, when devotion to the Virgin had become specially prominent; the Crusaders took the stories to the Middle East, where they were translated into Arabic in the middle of the thirteenth century, and via Egypt they reached Ethiopia at the beginning of the fifteenth. In the reign of Zar'a Yā'qob (1432–68) they were used for liturgical purposes, and by the sixteenth century, there was a recognised canon of 33 miracles in the Ethiopic version, and these were frequently illustrated. Many additional miracles were collected and appended in the various manuscripts, the present one including a total of 40. Among the illustrations is one from an earlier manuscript, of a fine walking Virgin and Child against a red background of vertical flower scrolls, as if it were wall decorations (f.180a); and a series of the Passion of Christ of 1668, such as the Deposition from the Cross, f.252a. Near the end of the volume, at f.266b–267a is a depiction of the Last Judgment. On the left, Christ is seated on an *alga*, or Ethiopian throne, with the souls of the righteous on his right, and of the damned on his left, while Satan below is trampled in everlasting fire. On the right, devils lead the souls of the wicked in chains into hellfire.

72 Miracles of the Blessed Virgin Mary. This vellum manuscript was written in a beautiful character of the latter part of the seventeenth century.

Or.635.

This volume contains 42 miracles, and has numerous illustrations. A typical fine one, with predominant reds, yellows and blacks, is at f.19b. It shows King David enthroned, playing a ten-stringed lyre (*kerar*) to accompany the Psalms; at his back an attendant holds an umbrella over him, while in his right hand he grasps a long sword.

73 Miracles of the Blessed Virgin Mary. Vellum manuscript of the late seventeenth century.

Or.645.

A charming picture from this collection illustrates at ff.49b–50a, the 'Miracle of Zacharias': every day he crowned Mary's picture with a garland of roses, which he gathered in the wilderness. One day he could not find any, and prayed humbly to Mary, who appeared to him with a train of angels, and plucked his prayers from his mouth in the form of roses. A band of robbers who had followed Zacharias, saw the miracle and became monks. The various incidents from the story are shown in succession in the picture.

74 Miracles of the Blessed Virgin Mary, Jesus and Saints. Vellum manuscript, written in a large fine character in the beginning of the eighteenth century.

Or.649.

Among the miracles illustrated in this volume is one at ff.49b–50a. of the 'Three Shipwrecked Arabs'. When they were in danger of drowning, two of them prayed to Mary to save them, vowing to become Christians when they reach an island; but the third blasphemes and is swallowed by a crocodile. The two survivors redeem their vows by bringing gifts of a bale of cloth and a block of dates to the church.

75–
76 Miracles of the Blessed Virgin Mary. This small manuscript on vellum is written in a good hand of the eighteenth century. It is profusely illustrated and bound in leather on wooden boards, with blind-tooling of traditional cross design; it is provided with a *māhdar*, or protective satchel, with linear designs of crosses in four panels.

Add.24188.

This volume begins with hymns and tracts; the main part contains the traditional 33 Miracles of Mary. At ff.26b–27a is the 'Miracle of Dexius, Bishop of Teltelya', this being the Ethiopic rendering of the name of St Ildefonsus, or Alphonsus, Archbishop of Toledo, who lived from 607 to 667. Among his works was *De Virginitate S. Mariae.* in praise of the Virgin, to whom he was greatly devoted. Medieval artists in Europe frequently depicted him, when he appeared to them, presenting him with a chasuble. It is an elaboration of this story which is shown in the Ethiopic volume: Mary was so pleased when he wrote his book, that she gave him a throne and a robe, warning that no-one else might use them. When he died, his successor announced that he would wear the robe and sit on the throne, but Mary sent the angel Raguel to strike him down.

77 Nagara Māryām. The history and miracles of the Blessed Virgin Mary. This is a vellum manuscript, written in a fine hand for 'Īyāsū II (1730–55), profusely illustrated.

Or.607.

This work is arranged for the twelve months of the year, and is also popularly known as the Gospel of the Mother, or 'called in the Egyptian tongue the Little Gospel'. At ff.16b–17a are scenes relating to Herod and the infant Jesus: Herod sends his army to Bäretas;

the Holy Family flee to Egypt; and the angel appearing to them.

78 The Degua. This is the Hymnbook of the Ethiopian Church for the whole of the year, and has musical notation. It is written in a small regular character on vellum in three columns, and is dated 1735.

Or.584. (Plates 28, 29)

This work is traditionally ascribed to the Abuna, or Metropolitan Yārēd, Archbishop of Axum in the sixth century, who is credited with the invention of Ethiopian music. However, the earliest version certainly known belongs to the fifteenth century, and an abridgment was made during the reign of Sarsa Dengel (1563–97). At f.232a, Yared is pictured as a *dabtara* or cantor, holding a sistrum and a staff, outside a small circular Ethiopian church, with the ostrich eggs on the roof as a symbol of life. At f.154b is shown the Abuna Takla Haymanot, the reforming Archbishop of the mid-thirteenth century during the time of the Emperor Yekuno Amlak. Takla Haymanot founded the monastery at Debra Libanos, whose Prior is the premier monk of Ethiopia and confessor and adviser of the Emperor. Later he became an ascetic living in a spiked cell, and is revered as a national hero.

79 Tabiba Tabiban. Vellum manuscript, written in two columns of eight lines in a fine hand in red and black, of the eighteenth century.

Or.590. (Plate 30)

The long hymn of the title is followed by a collection of stanzas, each addressed to a different angel, saint or martyr. The draftsmanship of the illustrations is very good, the pictures being presented panoramically, in some of which God is shown presiding in a garland of clouds. The artist took frequent delight in portraying gruesome detail. Among interesting scenes are those at ff.8b–9a, of the Flood, in which the successive scenes show God speaking to Noah; the building of the Ark; the animals entering; people drowning, and Noah blessing Shem. At f.10a, the Tower of Babel, a foreman directs while workmen hew stone and climb ladders on the tower, and God surveys the scene. At f.15b, the Children of Israel cross the Red Sea; to the left below, Pharaoh, with turbaned and bearded Egyptians and their horses are drowning, while Moses in patriarchal garb, with the Israelites, waits on land, and God looks on above.

80 Dersana Mikael. Discourses for the festivals of the Archangel Michael. This small vellum manuscript was written by two hands, the first of the seventeenth century, the other (from f.155) of the eighteenth. The older portion of the volume contains many pictures in outline; the scribe's name was Abraham.

Or.609.

The earlier part contains twelve discourses, to be read at the commemoration of St Michael on the twelfth day of each of the Ethiopian months. A good example of the outline drawings may be seen at ff.68b–69a, which show priests playing sistrum and drums in church, and a baptism. The later part contains an account of twelve Miracles of St Michael.

81 Dersana Mikael. A vellum manuscript written in a fine hand of the eighteenth century.

Or.614.

These discourses for the feasts of St Michael for each monthly commemoration, have a miracle and an extract from the Synaxarium appended to each. The latter part of the book has hymns to the Archangels Michael, Raphael and Gabriel. At f.43b are pictures of two of the national saints of Ethiopia: St Takla Haymanot, who in the thirteenth century played the major role in reorganizing the Church under the Emperor Yekuno Amlak, and then retired to a hermit's cell, where he meditated standing for 27 years till one leg atrophied. Legend tells he was given three pairs of wings when on one occasion he had to descend a sheer cliff face from a monastery, when the rope broke. The other popular local saint shown is St Gabra Manfas Qeddus, whose life was like that of St Francis of Assisi; he wore a robe of hair, or feathers, and is here seen with lions and leopards at his feet.

82 Dersana Mikael. Vellum manuscript written in a fine hand at the beginning of the eighteenth century.

Or.615.

This volume contains the discourses and miracles for the feasts of St Michael, followed by those for St Gabriel and St Raphael, and hymns of praise to them. At f.103b, at the opening of the section relating to St Gabriel, is a miniature of the Annunciation, in which the owner, or donor, of the volume is shown lying prostrate in prayer at Mary's feet. Throughout the book, the first owner's name is erased, and another, woman's name (who owned the work during the reign of King Bakafa, 1721–30) is substituted.

83 Apocryphal Acts of the Apostles. *Gadla Lawaryat.* This manuscript of vellum was written in a fair hand in the latter part of the eighteenth century and is profusely illustrated.

Or.685.

This work, which differs from the Greek apocryphal Acts, represents a tradition preserved in Coptic, Arabic and Ethiopic. The various Ethiopic manuscripts differ in detail, but generally consist of the preaching of each Apostle and Evangelist, and his martyrdom, related in separate chapters. At the beginning of the book, at ff.2b–3a is a miniature of St Gabra Manfas Qeddus, with two prostrate owners praying for his intercession. These are presumed to be Gabra Mikael and his wife Sahela Maryam, who with their daughter Hirula Dengal are named several times in the manuscript.

84 Acts of Saints and Martyrs. *Gadla Samā'tāt,* copied by the scribes Epiphanius and Yonas in a good hand of the eighteenth century; profusely illustrated.

Or.687–8.

Works of this class are arranged according to the festivals of the saints throughout the year. The present double volume contains 46 commemorations, and begins with two homilies of St John Chrysostom on the life and beheading of St John the Baptist. The acts of St Stephen conclude at f.43a with a miniature of his being stoned. Many of the saints included reflect the links with the Coptic Church, such as Menas, Mercurius and Peter of Alexandria.

85 Life and Acts of Takla Haymanot. *Gadla Takla Haymanot.* Vellum manuscript, copied in a fine hand at the beginning of the eighteenth century.

Or.721.

This life of the national saint contains many illustrations. At ff.31b–32a is shown his conception, birth and baptism. In the night of his conception, his mother, Igzi'o Haraya dreamt she saw a pillar of light on which perched many birds of different colours; this was interpreted that the child was to become a guide to the world, whose spiritual sons would venture far and wide. His father, Ṣaga Za-ab, in his dream saw the sun and bright stars from under their bed filling the sky, and an angel telling them of the marvellous son they were going to have.

86 Isaiah, Daniel and Apocryphal Books. Small vellum manuscript, written in more than one hand at the end of the eighteenth century.

Or.503. (Plate 31)

After the text of Isaiah, a list is given on f.32b. of books of the Bible as received by the Ethiopian Church. These include besides the Old and New Testament books, the Apocryphal books of the Septuagint, and others, of which some texts are given in this manuscript, including the Ascension of Isaiah, the Apocalypse of Baruch and the Apocalypse of Ezra. Another short work is the *Genealogy of the Fathers* at ff.33b–35b, from Adam, and through the line of Solomon and the Queen of Sheba to the Ethiopian emperors down to Fāsīladas, who ruled from 1632 to 1667. Ff.75b–76a. show King Yekuno Amlak, (1270–85), the restorer of the Solomonic line, receiving Muslim ambassadors. This late eighteenth century picture represents a high point in the later style of Gondar, which is often rather dark and heavy.

87 Kebra Nagast. The Glory of Kings. This is a well written manuscript on vellum of the first half of the eighteenth century.

Or.818.

This work is the chronicle of the kings of the Solomonid dynasty, embodying the essential elements of Ethiopian national and religious feelings. It includes the legend of the Queen of Sheba and Solomon, based on I Kings 10, verses 1–13, and the subsequent birth of her son Menelik, who went to Jerusalem to see his father, and to bring the Ark of Zion to Axum. From Menelik sprang the ruling family of Ethiopia, restored to power by Yekuno Amlak in 1270. At the end of the text at f.46b is a list of the kings of Ethiopia down to Amda Sion, who ruled from 1314 to 1344. The present manuscript contains several other texts, including historical works and homilies.

88 The History of King Lālībalā of Lāstā. *Gadla Lālībalā.* This well-written manuscript of the nineteenth century was prepared for Queen Walatta 'Iyasūs and her children; it has illustrations with Amharic inscriptions.

Or.718.

Lālībalā was the most famous king of the Zagwe dynasty which was in power from 1137 to 1268. He ruled from 1190–1225, and is famed for the construction of ten rock-cut churches in his dominion, at Roha, later renamed Lālībalā. This volume contains illustrations of incidents from his life. At f.39b Lālībalā as a child is seen distributing alms to the children of the poor (so in the Amharic caption; but the artist has painted lepers). At f.126a is a representation of one of the rock-cut churches, while at f.127b, Lālībalā is cutting the rock for their construction, a work which was continued at night by angels. After his death, King Lālībalā was considered a saint, and many ascetic feats and miracles were attributed to him.

AMULETS

When the nearest doctor, of any kind, may be four days' walk over the mountains, canyons and rushing rivers, an Ethiopian Christian suddenly stricken by an unknown frightening illness, may turn to ancient African or Middle Eastern magic which has been adapted to Christianity and more or less de-paganised. He will take the skin of a sheep (perhaps specially slaughtered as a kind of sacrificial meal) to the local *dabtara*, a lay official of the Church who can read and write (the ordained clergy tend to look down on these practices as useless superstition).

The *dabtara* will cut the skin into about three strips and sew them together into a scroll as long as the height of the patient. On this he will write various traditional prayers, calling on God, Jesus, Mary, the angels, the saints, the martyrs, the holy cross, the secret names of God – to save and protect the bearer (named) from specific illnesses, pains, evil spirits, devils, spells, the evil eye, etc., and – if requested – to make him or her respected, or loved, or fertile, etc. The texts are well interspersed with magical abracadabra words and mystical signs and usually a good deal of space is filled with holy or magical pictures.

89 A very ancient example (perhaps third cen-
(A1) tury) from Egypt, in Coptic, on papyrus. Or.6796(1).

This was folded up small and carried about on the person.

Typically, the Ethiopian magical prayer roll is written partly in red ink – usually the first line or two of each new prayer, the bearer's name and names of God, Jesus, Mary and special saints. Common pictures include the Archangel Michael with drawn sword, and other angels; saints often mounted, fighting armed devils or leading them captive; animals especially lions and snakes; ornamental crosses, some developed into or adapted from eight-pointed-shapes with faces, but without mouths; criss-cross nets (or spiders' webs, or 'Solomon's net', to ensnare devils); and watchful faces and eyes as in ancient Egyptian tomb paintings.

The strip when finished will be rolled up and put inside a bamboo or leather tube, to be worn on the person by means of a leather strap.

90 A typical amulet tube, of leather or bamboo.
(A2) Or.5423, case. Men and horses and donkeys used to be festooned with strings of these tubes.

91 Or.12025. A typical scroll with five charac-
(A3) teristic magical pictures.

92 Or.12959. Another, with three magical pictures;
(A4) a tall St Michael, a mounted saint spearing a devil, and a cross.

93 Or.13227. An interesting cross.
(A5)

94 Or.11602. A highly stylised representation of a
(A6) four or six-winged angel (or heavenly beast, cf. Ezek. Chap. 1).

95
(A7) Or.5423. St Michael against a decorated background and the owner Walda Maryam praying prostrate at his feet. The text is written in alternating black and red squares.

96 Or.11764. Some unusual features here include
(A8) lotuses, Elijah's chariot of fire, and a centaur-like creature, besides two of the usual eight-pointed cross 'spider' designs.

97 Or.12859. A magnificent specimen that must
(A9) have belonged to a rich and powerful man. Containing prayers for gaining respect, favour and love, and for protection from enemies, lances and other weapons, it exhibits fourteen miniatures:

 1 Alexander the Great, enemy of devils.
 2 Two men playing great drums.
 3 Two angels leading Satan captive.
4–9 Mounted saints fighting demons (No. 6 is labelled 'St George')
 10 Two lions (apparently protective beasts).
 11 The Lamb of God.
 12 Solomon in his 'orbits'.
 13 Elijah's chariot of light.
 14 St Michael chastising the demon 'who tortures souls'.

98 This scroll was kept in a beautiful silver filigree
(A10) tube. Or.12859, case.

99 Or.11804. Six unusual magical pictures,
(A11) including lions and other beasts, with fertility symbols.

100 Or.3716C. A striking example, with magical
(A12) pictures at beginning and end, and two collections of protective persons and objects in
between.

> Picture No. 2 shows: St Fasiladas spearing Satan; St Raguel, the Archangel, spearing a
> dragon; Satan leading the souls of the wicked; and a lion.
> Picture No. 3 shows: the Cross, Satan, the Virgin Mary; a tabot (wood or stone slab
> representing the tablets of Moses, kept in the sanctuary of every church); the Saviour of
> the world under an umbrella; a man with a gun and a dagger.

101 For comparison, a Syriac amulet is shown.
(A13) Written on paper, it was folded up very small,
tied with linen thread, and wrapped in cloth or
leather to be carried about. Deposit 637.

103 Facsimile of another Syriac amulet containing
(A16) prayers for a successful pregnancy and deliv-
ery, with magical drawing.

102 (A14) and 103 (A15)
Syriac books of amulets. Or. 11370 and Or. 6673.

ETHIOPIAN OBJECTS

Items 104–9 are adjuncts to Church worship, now in the collections of the Department of Medieval and Later Antiquities, British Museum.

104 Processional Crosses
(a) Pierced bronze, sixteenth century or earlier.
MLA 68/10–1/16 (Plate 32)

The interlaced patterns derive from early Coptic influence. The inscription reads: 'This is the cross of our
Father, Takla Haymanot'.
(b) Pierced brass, eighteenth century of Gon-
darene type.
MLA 68/12/307

This cross is inscribed with the name of King Bakafa
(1721–30), and engraved with scenes of the Flagella-
tion, Ecce Homo, the Crucifixion, and Daniel in the
lions' den.

105 Tabot. A wooden block, designed and dedicated
for insertion into an altar, with crosses and
decoration in red, and an Ethiopic inscription.
MLA 68/10–5/9

106 Diptychs
(a) A small brass diptych, with a seventeenth century French enamel on the left, with an engraved
scene with Ethiopic inscription on the right.
MLA 68/10–1/7

(b) Nineteenth century diptych, with eight divi-
sions, including pictures of St Michael, St George
and the Dragon, Takla Haymanot, the Virgin and
Child and the Crucifixion.
MLA 1953/7–3/1

107 Thurible. A silver censer, with square bowl,
incised with decorative motifs, with a bud-shaped
bell at a corner (the other three are missing).
Similar bells were also commonly attached to the
censer chains.
MLA 68/12-30/4

108 Sistrum. This instrument is used in religious
processions, being held in the hand and moved
slowly with a flick of the wrist, to the rhythm of
chanting and drums.
MLA 93/11-11/169

(Compare the illustration of the Abuna Yared in
Cat.No.78 above.)

109 Chalice and Paten. Engraved silver, nineteenth
century. MLA 68/10–1/8, 11

These came from the palace at Gondar, and both are
inscribed with the name of Theodore, who reigned
from 1855 to 1868, as donor.

BLACK

SEA

GEORGIA

●Ghelat

●Kutaisi

Mtskheta● ●Djvari
●Tbilisi

A
R
M
E
N
I
A

LAKE SEVAN

●Ani
Etchmiadzin
Bagaran● ●Eravan

Mt Ararat ▲
16946 ft

●Manzikart

LAKE VAN

●Van

Achthamar

LITTLE ARMENIA
(scale as main map)

●Sis

●Tarsus

MEDITERRANEAN
SEA

Antioch●

*Sis is approximately
550 miles ESE of Etchmiadzin*

25   50   100 *miles*
25   50   100 *kms*

The boundaries shown are of modern Soviet Armenia and Georgia

5 Armenia and Georgia, with Little Armenia (Cilicia)

56

6

Armenian Christianity

Modern Armenia is a tableland bounded by the rivers Chorokh and Kura on the north-west and north, by the rivers Araxes and the Lake of Urmia on the east and by the mountains of Kurdistan and the valley of the Tigris on the south. Mountain ranges, with the majestic peak of Mt Ararat rising to a height of about 17,000 ft, run across the plateau in an east-west direction dividing the country into a number of separate basins. Each one of her powerful neighbours sought to control or possess this natural fortress. The political history of this area was dominated by the struggles between the Roman and Byzantine empires on the one side, the Sassanian and the Arab empires on the other; in more recent times it was the bone of contention between Persia and Turkey and between Turkey and Russia; Armenia was frequently the battlefield and almost always one of the targets.

THE HISTORY OF ARMENIA

Following the blending of Indo-European and Urartian elements late in the second millennium BC, Armenia emerged at about 600 BC as an ethnic group, whose kings were vassals of the rulers of ancient Persia; in the fourth century BC the conquests of Alexander the Great made most of Armenia part of his empire. The Armenians regained their independence under their resourceful King Artaxias (190–189 BC). The first Armenian sovereign state reached its highest point in the reign of Tigranes the Great (95–66 BC), but in the course of its encounter with Rome was compelled to give up most of its extensive conquests.

  For more than four centuries, the Arsacid kings of Armenia had to contend with the rivalries between Rome and Persia, who finally divided the country in AD 387. The Arsacid kings continued to rule under the suzerainty of Persia until AD 428, after which the country was governed by margraves appointed by Persia until the conquest of Armenia by the Arabs in AD 642. Invasions, persecutions and excessive taxation devastated and impoverished the country, while the wars between Byzantium and the Arabs further complicated the political situation. With the new successes of the Byzantine armies over the Arabs in the middle of the ninth century, the fear of new uprisings compelled the Arabs to adopt a more conciliatory policy towards Armenia. In 861 the caliph appointed Asot Bagraduni as Prince of Princes. Thus the Armenian monarchy was restored after a lapse of more than four centuries.

This period of Armenian history (861–1064) marked the apogee of material prosperity and cultural revival in Armenia. After the death of Gagik I (989–1020) the Armenian Bagraduni monarchy rapidly declined due to internal rivalries and with the desire of the Byzantine emperors to expand their borders in the west; while on the east the raids of Seljuk Turks increased intensively. The annexation of Armenia in 1045 under Constantine IX facilitated the Seljuk attack. Led by Alp Aslan, the Seljuk Turks invaded Armenia and took possession of the capital Ani in 1065, laid waste Cilicia and forced their way into Asia Minor. After the Byzantine disaster in Manazkert in 1071, Seljuk rule was firmly established in Armenia. The aftermath of the Seljuk conquest of Armenia was mass dispersion of its social and political élite to foreign lands.

The most important migration of Armenians was towards south-eastern Anatolia and in 1198 a new Armenian kingdom was established in Cilicia. Three centuries of effective political power, fighting against tremendous odds, opened a new chapter in the history of the people. The Crusades affected the destiny of the Cilician kingdom. Later the Mongols, on whom the Armenian kings had relied throughout in their struggle against the Sultan of Egypt, were converted to Islam, which meant that Armenia lost its ally. In 1375 the capital of Sis fell to the Egyptian Arabs and the last Armenian King Leo V (VI) was taken as a captive to Egypt. He was released after seven years through the intervention of John of Castile and Peter of Aragon, and died in Paris in 1393.

The destiny of the Armenian nation after the establishment of the Ottoman empire on the ruins of the Byzantine dominion in 1453 was an unhappy one. The Turco-Persian wars in the seventeenth century were particularly destructive. The Persian king Shah Abbas (1587–1629) forced tens of thousands of Armenians to settle in the suburbs of his new capital Isfahan in 1604–5. A well articulated cultural centre was created here which, in its turn, through trade created new Armenian communities in India and Indonesia. The period between 1895–1920 marks a crucial turning point in the modern history of the Armenians in the Ottoman empire. These years stand out as the tragic decades which ushered in a period of unrest and disturbances, causing deep national anxiety and anguish that did not end until the uprooting and extermination of the Armenian people in Asiatic Turkey in 1915. The story of this period culminated in the creation of the Armenian Soviet Republic in 1920.

Tradition has it that the Gospel was brought to these parts in the 60s of the first century AD by the apostles Thaddeus and Bartholomew, the first 'Illuminators' of Armenia. The number of converts to the new faith must have increased in the course of the second and third centuries, for there were persecutions under King Artases about 110, King Xosrov in about 230, and more started in 287 under King Tiridates, but in his reign Christianity finally triumphed and was declared the state religion by royal decree in 301 (some sources even claim 287). This makes Armenia the first country to have recognised Christianity officially, since Constantine's decree of 313 was only an edict of tolerance for the new faith.

St Gregory, the second 'Illuminator' of Armenia who was a laymen at the time, received episcopal consecration from Bishop Leontius, Archbishop of Caesarea and was elected Catholicos of all Armenians. The cathedral of Etchmiadzin was begun in the same year and completed in 303 on the spot where Gregory had had a vision, in which Christ appeared and ordered him to erect a church on the site of a Zoroastrian place of worship. The city is still the spiritual centre of Armenian Christianity, where every year pilgrims come in their thousands to the place where their church was founded 1,600 years ago.

After the year 373 open canonical ties with Caesarea were severed, by which time the national church had become sufficiently mature and strong. Patristic works were translated into Armenian: the writings of St Basil, Gregory the Thaumaturgos, Gregory of Nazianzus, Gregory of Nyssa, John Chrysostom, Athanasius, Cyril of Alexandria, Cyril of Jerusalem; these writings were predominantly Alexandrian in their approach to Christological problems of the time. The Armenian church recognizes the doctrinal and canonical validity of the first three Ecumenical councils, of Nicea (325), Constantinople (381) and Ephesus (431) as adequate for 'the basis of life and guide to the path leading to God' and rejects the decisions of the council of Chalcedon (451). Because of this rejection, both Orthodox and Roman Catholic churches have erroneously considered the Armenian church as being Monophysite. The Armenian church has always rejected the mingling or the confusion of the two natures in Christ and recognised in Him a divine and a human nature, adopting the definition 'One nature in the Incarnate God'. It is for this reason that the Armenian church celebrates the Baptism (the manifestation of Divinity) and the Birth (manifestation in the flesh) of Christ on the same day (6 January), whereas the Greeks and others celebrate the same events on two separate days (25 December and 6 January).

The whole nation having identified its destiny with the Christian faith had to struggle hard for the survival of that faith. The first real test came in the second half of the fifth century, when the Persians took forceful measures to impose Mazdaism upon the Armenians. The Church, the nobility and the people rallied round Vardan

Mamikonean and waged the decisive battle in the plains of Avarayr in 451. Against superior forces of the Persians and in spite of their valour, the Armenians were defeated. The guerilla warfare continued until 484 when the Persians were obliged to come to terms with the Armenians. Freedom of religious worship was restored, the independence of Armenia recognised.

The Armenian church today with its spiritual centre in Etchmiadzin, with the Catholicosate established in Lebanon in 1929, with the patriarchal seats in Jerusalem and Constantinople, looks after the religious and national aspirations of five million Armenians scattered throughout the world, in the Middle East, Western Europe, North and South America, Egypt, Iran, India, Australia and New Zealand.

LITERATURE

The national consciousness aroused by the conversion to Christianity was reinforced in the early fifth century by the invention of the Armenian alphabet, an event of foremost importance for the entire history of the Armenian people and church. Until then Armenian was a spoken language; the religious services were performed in Syriac in Persian Armenia, or in Greek in Byzantine Armenia. The danger of assimilation on the one hand and dechristianisation on the other made the need of a national script urgent. The task was entrusted to the learned priest Mesrop Mastoc' who, after long research in the capitals of Amid, Edessa and Samosata, devised an alphabet admirably suited to the Armenian language, consisting of thirty-six letters. The great task was 'to teach, write and translate' the scriptures, the liturgy, the canons, the important writings of Greek and Syrian Fathers and to train scholars, so Mesrop Mastoc' sent students for further study to Edessa, Caesarea and Constantinople.

The first book to be translated was the Bible, first from the Syriac and then retranslated from the Greek by the Catholicos Sahak Partev from the Septuagint version. 'Learn wisdom and the precepts . . .' (Proverbs 1: 2–7) were the first words, written on parchment, pointing to the path of development which Armenian literature followed. Many of the translations from Syriac and Greek made in the course of the two centuries after the invention of the alphabet form the 'Golden Age' of Armenian literature. In several instances these translations preserved the texts of the Greek and Syriac Church Fathers whose originals were lost, such as the *Chronicle* of Eusebius, the *Commentaries* on the Benediction of Moses by Hippolytus, and the *Refutation of the Definition* of the Council of Chalcedon by Timothy Aelurus. Besides the religious writings, secular texts were translated, such as the Alexander *Romance* of the Pseudo Callisthenes, the *Grammar* of Dionysius Thrax and numerous philosophical writings.

Original literature included the *Histories* of Agatangelos, Koriwn, Elisē, Lazar P'arp'ec'i and Movses Xorenac'i. Theological writings were mainly hagiogaphy,

60

homilies and commentaries. Among poetic works the pride of place belongs to *The Book of Prayers* written in 1002 by the mystic poet Grigor Narekac'i. Each of the ninety-five poems begin with the words 'From the depth of the heart a soliloquy with God' and give expression to the mystical meditations of a deeply religious and fervent man. The hymns and religious poems of Nerses Snorhali (1101–73) reveal a more serene though equally devout nature. His elegy on *The Fall of Edessa* shows how deeply the disaster affected Armenians in Cilicia. In the first part of the poem Edessa personified calls on the Sees of the five ancient patriarchates – Jerusalem, Rome, Constantinople, Alexandria and Antioch, to lament her fate. The elegy on the *Fall of Jerusalem* composed on the same pattern by Grigor Tla is equally well known. Most of the works mentioned here briefly have been translated in English, French and other languages.

MANUSCRIPT MINIATURES AND ILLUMINATIONS

The oldest specimens of Armenian miniatures consist of four representing The Annunciation to Mary, The Annunciation to Zachariah, The Adoration of the Magi, and The Baptism of Christ. These fragments of a perished manuscript dated in the seventh century are inserted at the end of the famous Etchmiadzin Gospels, written in 989. The oldest manuscript with miniatures and an exact date is the Gospel Book of Queen Mlk'e written in 862. Many Armenian manuscripts perished through foreign invasions, warfare and persecution. According to a contemporary witness, during the Seljuk invasion of Armenia in 1170 more than ten thousand manuscripts were destroyed.

The vast production of manuscripts can partly be explained by the supreme importance Armenians attached to them; the act of copying, of commissioning a manuscript to be written, or even redeeming a manuscript from the hands of the infidel, was considered a deed of piety, an 'imperishable treasure set up in heaven'. Hence scribes throughout the centuries devoted their whole lives to the task of copying chronicles, religious texts, works on history, philosophy, astronomy, medicine, law and grammar. They were often poor and destitute, but they worked with extraordinary fervour and asked for little in return for their labours. One such recorded his feelings: 'O brethren, I beseech you to remember me the wretched scribe Gregory, who transcribed this book and drew the pictures and adorned it with gold and colours'. Another said: 'I know only too well that there are countless imperfections in this manuscript, but I have done what I could. My hand was trembling and I could scarcely see – my first finger was paralysed and I had to use the middle one. What a calamity. I have been working for 42 years now and nothing like this has ever happened before. I am ashamed. Please forgive me . . .' But a sentence that best illustrates the spirit in which the copyist worked is: 'Long after my hand has withered and the body itself turned to dust, this writing shall continue to be read'.

At a rough estimate, about 24,000 Armenian manuscripts have survived to the present day. The most important collections are in Armenian Institutions such as the Matenadaran (Erevan), St James's Monastery (Jerusalem), the Libraries of the Armenian Catholic communities of Venice and Vienna and others in the major libraries of Europe and America. Generally illuminated manuscripts have pictures of fifteen Christian themes, ten of them of full-page dimensions; each of the Gospels has a frontispiece consisting of two full-page miniatures, the one placed on the left representing the particular Evangelist and the page on the right being occupied by a headpiece dominating the first lines of the text. The decorations consist of marginal ornaments, canon tables, small miniature portraits of saints and other geometrical, animal and floral motifs. The full page illuminations represent the major events in Christ's life such as the Nativity, the Adoration, Entry into Jerusalem, the Crucifixion, the Resurrection and the Ascension.

Besides their textual and artistic merits Armenian manuscripts are also important for their colophons which developed a unique tradition in that besides recording the facts surrounding the circumstances of the production of individual manuscripts, they also included valuable contemporary information on a broad range of subjects such as natural disasters, invasions and historical events. These serve as primary sources for the study of the history of not only Armenia, but also of the Middle East. This is true of manuscripts written in localities as far apart as Central Asia, Iran, Constantinople, Europe, the Crimea, Caucasia, Egypt and India. The chronological data in the colophons is provided by various Armenian and foreign calendars. The majority use the Great Armenian Era which began in 552.

Examples of Armenian manuscript bindings are described at nos. 157–8. See also no. 134 for a gilt répoussé binding.

ARTS IN THE SERVICE OF THE CHURCH

In the history of Armenian culture architecture holds a special place. According to a recent view: 'of all the border countries of the empire, Armenia is the only one to deal with Byzantine architecture on an equal footing'. The church of The Holy Cross built in 915–921 by the architect Manuel on the Island of Aghtamar is unique for the reliefs of biblical scenes running around all its façades. Various styles are to be seen in the numerous churches of Ani, capital of the Bagraduni kingdom. The cathedral was built between 989–1001.

In the domain of sculpture, the Armenians concentrated on friezes and bas-reliefs which were carved on churches. The memorial cruciform stones called Khachkar (Stone Cross) constitute the most original expression of Armenian sculpture. They were funerary or votive stone crosses carved with figures of Christ, the Virgin and St

John and other scenes from the Old and New Testaments. They were erected in memory of victories, the dedication of a new bridge or village and frequently they were also incorporated into the walls of buildings, churches and cemeteries.

Armenian religious music has a long history. The Khaz (neume) notation of Armenian religious music has been preserved in many ancient manuscripts from the ninth and tenth centuries which contain the texts of the Armenian Liturgy, the hymns, chants and canticles. The Khazes are written in one colour above the lines of the text. Some of the medieval Armenian universities which were attached to the churches and monasteries had a special Department of Music, where the knowledge of the Khaz system of notation and theory of religious music was an essential condition of priesthood.

110 Khachkar. Armenian Stone Cross. Thirteenth century. Presented by His Holiness Vasken I, Catholicos of all Armenians.

(Plate 19)

Memorial crosses became a special feature of Armenian artistic expression, with their elaborate carvings, including figures of Christ, the Virgin Mary and saints in niches, subsidiary crosses, decorated medallions, interlaced designs and inscriptions in Armenian.

111 The Four Gospels. Preceded by the Letter of Eusebius to Carpianus, and the Ammonian Canons, this manuscript on vellum was copied in 1181 in the monastery of Drazark (Cilician Armenia), and was illuminated by the priest Xacatur. The hand is a regular neat uncials (Erkatagir). The binding is oriental dark leather over boards with a flap; both covers were originally adorned with metal crosses.

Or.81.

The volume includes at f.1b a miniature of Samuel, Primate of the Order, presenting the book to Christ. At the beginning of each Gospel are full-page miniatures of the several Evangelists seated writing, and on the facing pages, the commencement of the text has a well executed head-piece in green, red and gold, surmounted by birds. Each Gospel begins with a festooned initial capital almost as tall as the page; the first few letters are written on a blue background in large gold uncials, and there are further decorations in the text. According to the colophon the manuscript was written by 'Toros, an unintelligent scribe, during the reign of the Catholicios Gregory IV (1173–1193), and Prince Ruben II, King of Cilician Armenia (1174–1185)'.

112 The Avag Vänk Gospels. A large vellum manuscript of the Four Gospels, copied in 1200–1, by the monk Vardan at the Avag Vänk monastery near Erzincan on the upper Euphrates in Eastern Turkey, during the patriarchate of the Catholicos Gregory VI (1194–1203).

Or. 13654 (Plate 11)

This is the most important Armenian manuscript in the British Library collection. It is beautifully illuminated, and has marginal notes vividly reflecting the history and sufferings of the Armenian people. The text is written in ink in heavy majestic uncials (Erkatagir), and the title page of each Gospel has a fine head-piece of interlaced design, supporting peacocks and other

birds, elaborate initial letters and the symbols of the four Evangelists: angel, lion, bull and eagle. The binding is seventeenth century, of tooled brown calf, and on the front cover are five silver crosses around a central crucifix, with inscriptions in memory of the owner of that time and his deceased relatives.

113 The Four Gospels. This paper manuscript was written in the round hand (Boloragir), for the Catholicos Constantine I (1221–67) at Hromkla in Cilician Armenia.

Chester Beatty Library, Dublin. MS.558.

The Catholicos was patron of the famous painters Kirakos, Hohannes and Toros Roslin, but the name of the artist of the present manuscript is unknown. At ff.3v–4a is the *Letter of Eusebius*, with a head-piece enclosing portraits of Eusebius and Carpianus. The capitals of the columns are formed by lions standing on all fours. Two peacocks drawn above the rectangle stand at the sides of a gold vase out of which one of them is drinking. This manuscript is an outstanding example of Cilician art of the thirteenth century.

114 New Testament. This vellum manuscript was copied in an elegant medium-sized round hand (Boloragir) in double columns in the 'Armenian era 729 [AD 1280], in the metropolis of Sis [the capital of the Armenian Kingdom of Cilicia], under the shelter of the Church of the Holy Spirit', by Stephanos of Vakhay. It was restored by Mesrop, from the famous school of Khizan in Ispahan during the reign of Shah Abbas. It has an oriental binding of brown leather, with an ornate cross pricked out on the front cover.

Add.18549 (Colour Plate III)

After the Gospels, the order of books, Pauline Epistles, Acts, General Epistles, is that of Euthalius, whose testimonies are given in the margins. The five full-page portraits of the Evangelists, and of Peter and Paul at the beginning of the Epistles, were added in Ispahan in the seventeenth century, as were the pictures of saints in the margins of Acts and of the Catholic Epistles. The rest of the illuminations, including head-pieces, decorative letters and marginal ornamentations of birds apparently belong to the thirteenth century. The manuscript originally belonged to Toros, son of Aushin, brother of King Ketum I of Cilicia, who died in 1289.

115 The Four Gospels. A vellum manuscript, 'copied in the twelfth year of the reign of King Leo in the monastery of Drazark . . . in memory of the *vardapet* [priest] Toros and his family', 1282. The scribe is Barsel and the artist Hovhannes. The text is in a middle-sized, elegant round hand (Boloragir).

Or.5626

This volume is richly ornamented with ornate head-pieces, capitals, and marginal arabesques. Each Gospel is preceded by a portrait of the Evangelist, and the text begins with letters fashioned from the Evangelist's symbol (an angel, a lion, etc.). The dominant colours are blue, red and black and for the first time gold is also lavishly used. The king referred to in the colophon is Leo III of Cilician Armenia (1270–89). In 1425, the book was repaired, 'after it had fallen into the hands of enemies'.

116 Four Gospels. This volume is on oriental cotton paper, and was copied in a uniform round hand (Boloragir) by the priest Karapet, in 1304 in Cilicia, during the reign of King Het'um II (1289–1307) and the Catholicos Gregory VII.
Bodleian Library, Oxford. Armenian MS. D3.

This manuscript has a full set of Gospel illustrations at the beginning, including at f.6b–7a the Burial of Christ, with St Mary, St John and Joseph of Arimathea in attendance, and the Descent into Hell, where Christ is seen with Solomon and David. The binding is elaborate, with silver round-headed nails, some stones and on the upper cover an engraved Persian seal with an Armenian inscription in memory of Ter Yohanes and his wife, dated 1694, and further commemorative crosses on the lower cover.

117 The Four Gospels. Two fragments from a Gospel book written in 1311 by the priest Dser and illuminated by the deacon Toros. The miniatures origianlly belonged to Gospel MS I of the Church of the Theotokos in Tabriz in Iran.
Chester Beatty Library, Dublin. MS.559
(Plate 14)

1 *The Dormition of the Virgin.* The Virgin, with arms folded lies on the bed, while Christ with both hands raises her soul. Nearby is an angel with incense box and two Apostles, while the remaining Apostles are grouped on the right; in the foreground stands a deacon with a censer. This subject was first treated in Armenian art in the thirteenth century.

2 *Christ in Judgment.* The Virgin and the Apostle John stand in prayer on either side of the seated Christ, from whose throne emerge the Four Beasts, and the two Seraphim of the vision of Isaiah, while two archangels in the foreground are from the book of Daniel. The whole composition represents an original treatment of the subject.

118 Psalter. This vellum manuscript is written in a clear and elegant round hand (Boloragir), and was copied 1312–21 by the scribe Yohan, and illuminated by Sargis Picak, the most celebrated artist of fourteenth-century Cilician Armenia, active 1312–48.

Or.13804

A memorial notice of f.258 refers to Leo as King in 1283, that is Leo III (1269–89). The manuscript is decorated throughout with geometrical and floral designs, and capitals in red ink, and the Canon Tables have ornate head-pieces supporting birds and other designs. At f.2b there is a full-page miniature of the Virgin and Child with, at the bottom left-hand corner, a lay figure robed and kneeling, with his hands extended in prayer and the legend: 'O Mother of God, the Baron Hanes, the Chancellor, prays to thee for his soul'.

119 The Four Gospels. This manuscript on vellum was copied in a clear Boloragir hand and illuminated in the monastery of Gladzor in Cilician Armenia by Toros of Taron in 1321. It has illuminated Canon Tables, full-page portraits of the Evangelists (St Luke is missing), with full-page headings to the Gospels. It was restored at New Julfa, Ispahan in 1621, and has a tooled leather binding.
Add.15411 (Plates 12,13)

Toros of Taron was the best known Armenian artist of the fourteenth century. The opening of St Mark's Gospel is particularly attractive, the portrait on the left showing him seated at work in his scriptorium against an architectural background, while the heading of the text is a miniature of the Virgin and Child, flanked by angels, and a winged lion couchant below precedes the ornate lettering. The manuscript was written 'in a bitter age, when the race of the Archers [Seljuks] exercised tyranny over the whole land of the Armenians and Iberians', during the reign of the Cilician Armenian King Leo V, of the Rubenian dynasty, who ruled from 1320 to 1342. This was one of a number of manuscripts acquired by wealthy Armenian merchants of New Julfa in the seventeenth century.

120 The Four Gospels. This vellum manuscript is written in a round hand (Boloragir), and was illuminated at Sis, the capital of Cilician Armenia in 1329 by the 'unworthy and humble priest Sargis' Picak, for King Leo V.

Chester Beatty Library, Dublin. MS.561
(Plate 15)

At f.95b is a portrait of St Mark seated before a table, while the hand of God appears from the sky in blessing from the upper right-hand corner of the picture. This is a good example of the art of Sargis Picak, the foremost Cilician painter of the fourteenth century.

121 The Four Gospels. This manuscript on oriental cotton paper, was copied in a near round hand (Boloragir), by the monk Nerses in the monastery of St Cyriacus and the Holy Cross at the foot of Mount Bethno in the province of Ekeliac' (Erzincan in Eastern Turkey), in 1335. It has an oriental binding of tooled leather.

Bodleian Library, Oxford. Armenian MS. D.4

The ornaments throughout are remarkable for their neatness and beauty, and include Canon Tables with decorated arcades and birds above, and full page portraits of the Evangelists, and decorated headings to the Gospels, that of St Mark at ff.105b–106a being specially beautiful.

122 The Four Gospels. This manuscript is of fine vellum, written in a small round hand (Bolaragir), by the artist Avag, who was active between the years 1329–58, principally at Sultaniya in north-west Iran.

Or.5304

The artist has signed his name at the end of the Letter of Eusebius on f.2. He illustrates the Gospel stories in great detail, with miniatures introduced into the text in a way often found in Cilician manuscripts of the thirteenth century. This important work of a well-known painter contains many illustrations, unfortunately in a poor state of preservation. For instance, f.38b has 22 lines of text in the top left hand corner; the rest of the page is a composite miniature, in which the principal subject is the Nativity, Mother and Child in the centre, with ox and ass, the Wise Men to the left, angels above, and a small scene of the infant Christ being washed at the foot of the picture.

123 The Four Gospels. This manuscript was written on stout oriental paper, in a large round hand (Boloragir), in the province called Balu in 1437, at the monastery of St George, 'during the bitter and cruel time, when untimely death at the hands of unbelievers, made it impossible for the priests to eat bread'. The scribe, Avetik, completed the manuscript when Hamzah Sultan was governor of Mesopotamia, and Constantine VI of Vakha was Catholicos of Cilician Armenia (1429–39). It is bound in leather, and formerly had metal ornaments.

Or.2668

The manuscript contains a full set of illustrations of the life of Christ. The miniature at f.3b of the Transfiguration with Christ standing in a lunette, in an attitude of blessing, flanked by Elijah and Moses, with Peter, James and John in semi-prostrate positions below, well demonstrates the persistence of the artistic presentation of this subject in the east from the earliest times.

124 Prayer Roll. This was written at Kaffa in 1456, and contains extracts from the Four Gospels, and the prayers of St Grigor Narekac'i, and has several miniatures, including one of St Sarkis and St Gregory the Illuminator.

Or.11264

The date 301 is usually given for the proclamation of Christianity as the state religion of Armenia, when the royal family had been converted by St Gregory, who became the patron saint of the Armenian Apostolic Church, and founder of the patriarchal see of Etchmiadzin.

125 Bible. This manuscript of the Old and New Testaments was copied perhaps in the fifteenth century, by the scribe Pilippos from an earlier one dated 1198. It includes the original colophon, which states that Jerusalem had been taken by the Muslims, and that in 1198, Leo II, Prince of Armenia, had been crowned King of Cilicia with a crown of precious stones sent from 'New Rome' by the Emperor Alexius III.

Or.8833

The manuscript has several full-page miniatures, including at ff.2b–3a, on the left, God the Creator, Adam and Eve in the Garden, and their expulsion, and on the right, an elaborate head-piece with the Virgin and Child in a roundel flanked by angels, and small roundels at the corners with the Evangelists and their beasts. Throughout the text there are marginal decorations, including birds and ornamental spearheads, decorated headings and capitals, and small figures of the Prophets, and in the Gospels, illustrations of Christ's healing miracles.

126 The Lives of the Fathers. The manuscript is on glazed paper, and is copied in round hand (Boloragir) by the scribe Sahak for Bishop Mkrtich in 1489 in the town of Karkar, south of Lake Van.

Chester Beatty Library, Dublin. MS. 602
(Plate 18)

A miniature of St Gregory the Illuminator, and King Tiridates appear on f.46. This illustration is associated with the feast of St John the Baptist, instituted by St Gregory, the text recalling the return of the relics of John, the miracles which took place, and the destruction of pagan temples. The miniature represents King Tiridates on horseback, meeting St Gregory who converted him to Christianity. The monster being trampled, and the architectural setting refer to incidents in the saint's life, the latter being a vision of four columns with crosses above them, representing the four principal churches of Armenia, including that of Etchmiadzin.

127 The Four Gospels. Manuscript on oriental cotton paper, copied in a regular round hand (Boloragir) by Grigor of Aghtamar in the Church of the Holy Cross, on the island of Aghtamar in Lake Van, in 1497 during the patriarchate of Atom.

Bodleian Library, Oxford. Armenian MS. E.1

The manuscript contains a full set of Gospel illustrations at the beginning of the text, some with red backgrounds, decorated Canon Tables, portraits of the Evangelist and elaborate headings to the Gospel texts.

128 The Four Gospels. This manuscript on stout oriental paper was copied by the scribe Karapet, 'from a choice and accurate archetype' in Bzunik, now called Xlat, north of Lake Van, during the reign of Sultan Sulaiman I (1520–66), in 1542.

Or.2707

Following the practice developed in Armenia during the fourteenth century, illustrations of symbolical scenes from the Old Testament and major episodes from the life of Christ are grouped together in a set at the beginning of the volume. Two themes newly included in this particular volume are the Tree of Jesse

as the symbol of the Incarnation, and the Vision of Ezekiel, representing the Second Coming of Christ. Among the New Testament scenes are the Entry into Jerusalem, with Zaccheus shown in the tree; and the Washing of the Disciples' Feet.

129 Bible History. This vellum manuscript was written in a small regular Boloragir hand by the scribe Hovhannes, son of Tjanibek, assisted by Aslan, in 1601 at Amida (now Diyarbakir in eastern Turkey), for Bishop Serapion of Edessa.

Chester Beatty Library, Dublin. MS. 551

The text narrates the history of the families from Adam to Jesus, and the relationships of the Old and New Testaments. The initials of the chapters are in animal or floral form. At ff.4b–5a is The Garden of Eden. The image of Paradise of the head-piece shows the four rivers swinging upward from the rocky foreground, and shows also the legendary six monks who set out to find the Garden. This theme is sometimes shown in Armenian manuscripts of the Lives of the Fathers. The manuscript is of rare interest both for its content and for its presentation of Old Testament illustrations.

130 The Four Gospels. These Gospels were copied in the city of Sous (Ispahan), Iran, by the scribe and illuminator Mesrop, 'with lovely colours, gold and lapis lazuli, and all sorts of pigments, as a goodly memorial', in 1607. It has a tooled leather binding.

Or.5737 (Plate 22)

Mesrop, a pupil of Martiros, is a representative of the well-known school of Khizan. The series of miniatures and the numerous marginal decorations are executed in green, red, yellow and blue. Seventeen full-page miniatures, mostly of the life of Christ in a somewhat severe hieratic style, begin the work, and the chief figures are set in a gold background and framed in a border of interlacing lines. This set is followed in the customary way with illuminated Canon Tables, and each Gospel has a portrait of the Evangelist facing a full-page illuminated heading of the text.

131 The Lives of the Fathers. This fine manuscript was written in a clear notary's hand (Notagir), by the scribes Hovhannes, Minas and Melkon in 1614, in Tigranakert, in Mesopotamia, during the reign of Sultan Ahmad I (1603–17), and Shah Abbas I of Persia (1587–1629).

Add. 27301

In Armenian, there are two recensions of *The Lives of the Fathers*, one apparently begun in the fifth century and added to from the eighth to the thirteenth; and the other of the fourteenth. This manuscript begins with an elegant head-piece with marginal ornaments, and has 25 illuminations of saints illustrating the text.

132 Psalter and Hymnal. This small paper manuscript is written in a fine notary's hand (Notagir). The manuscript has no colophon, but a note at f.58a has: 'I beseech you to remember the scribe Yakob'. It was copied in the seventeenth century, and has a tooled leather binding, and was brought from Constantinople by R. Curzon in 1837.

Or.8831

The hymns of the Armenian Church are here arranged according to the major dominical feasts, with 20 miniatures illustrating these, the subjects mostly being similar to those found in Gospel sets, and all depicted with gold backgrounds. An important feature of the manuscript is the inclusion of the old Armenian system of musical notation called Khaz (neumes), which was devised in the fifth century and continued in use till the second half of the nineteenth.

133 Lives of the Saints. This richly decorated manuscript was copied in 1652 in Constantinople by the scribe Xacatur, during the reign of the Catholicos Pilippos I of Albak (1633–55), and the sultanate of Muhammad IV (1648–87). The artist, Yovsep, signed himself in red ink in the lower margin of f.575a as 'the most insignificant of drudges'.

Or.12550 (Plate 23)

This menologion, or collection of lives of the saints and martyrs venerated by the Armenian Church, is artistically the best of four in the British Library collection, the others being dated 1488, 1701 and 1810. The miniature at f.257b, occupying the full page, is divided into three panels, the two above showing two stages, or perhaps two versions, of the Annunciation, the second with an architectural background, while below the Adoration of the Magi depicts the Holy Family to the left and the three kings to the right in attitudes of spiritual tranquillity, in a setting of rocky countryside.

134 The Four Gospels. This small vellum manuscript is written in a double column in clear round hand (Boloragir), in 1680.

Or.13808

The work is extensively illuminated, with Canon Tables decorated in gold, blue and red, with lions, birds and allegorical beasts. Each Gospel has a full page portrait of the Evangelist, and there are 56 smaller marginal miniatures. The book is bound in parcel gilt repoussé, the upper cover depicting a Nativity scene, with an inscription in Armenian from St Luke, while the lower cover has a representation of the Resurrection. The spine is elaborately ornamented with portraits of the Fathers of the Church, inscribed by the artist, Malxas Karapet, in Armenian, stating that he had created this work in the city of Caesarea in the Armenian era 1140 (AD 1691).

135 The Four Gospels. This manuscript is copied on fine vellum in a small round hand (Boloragir) in 1683.

Or.5449

The 16 miniatures on ff.1–16 are a typical set, and include the Annunciation, the Adoration of the Magi, the Presentation in the Temple, the Baptism of Christ, the Transfiguration, the Raising of Lazarus, the Entry into Jerusalem, Christ washing the Disciples' Feet, the Betrayal, Crucifixion, Burial, Resurrection, Christ in Glory, the Assumption of the Virgin, the Second Advent (represented by the Mystic Cross, with four angels trumpeting), and the Last Judgment. The volume also has illuminated Canon Tables; portraits of the Evangelists; elaborate Gospel headings, and numerous marginal decorations of Christ, the Apostles, saints, birds amid foliage and fruit, heads of corn and other designs. Among those of Christ is one of Him blessing two children at f.196a.

7

Christianity in Georgia

U NLIKE the majority of the Eastern Christian peoples considered so far, the Georgians belong to the Eastern Orthodox rite, and have done so since the early seventh century. They are thus in communion with the Greek and Russian Churches, and this fact has played an important role in Georgia's cultural, intellectual and political history.

The Georgians are an ancient autochtonous population of the region immediately to the south of the main Caucasus range. About three-quarters of their territory is now contained within the boundaries of the Georgian Soviet Socialist Republic. However, substantial areas of south-western Georgia are now within the Turkish republic. These areas include Lazistan, which was part of the medieval kingdom of Lazica on the Black Sea coast. Also included within the boundaries of Turkey is the important region of Tao-Klarjeti, once the cradle of monastic culture in ninth-century Georgia, and a political centre from which the power of the Bagratid dynasty reached out to unify Georgia in the eleventh century.

ANCIENT CULTURE

The ancestors of the Georgians excelled in metal working and the ceramic arts, beginning about 3000 BC. These cultural traditions came to fruition in the rich civilizations of Colchis – famous for Medea and the Golden Fleece – and Iberia, further east towards the Caspian Sea. The Black Sea region of Georgia was colonized by the Milesians from Greece in the seventh century BC. Georgia was later conquered and annexed by Pompey, in 66–65 BC.

Before the introduction of Christianity, the Georgians evolved a complex system of pagan ritual and belief. Mithraism was widespread, as was the cult of sacred trees. The Iranian pantheon had many adepts, while early Christian hagiographic sources mention the cult of various local idols.

Even in those distant days, the Georgians enjoyed a high level of urban development, as well as evolving advanced agriculture. They were far from being illiterate. A number of inscriptions on metal and stone have been recovered, notably from the first three centuries AD, using both Greek and a local form of Aramaic, known as the Armazi script.

EARLY CHRISTIANITY IN GEORGIA

By the early fourth century, much of western Georgia had been evangelized by missionaires active in the Greek colonies along the Black Sea coast. The Council of Nicaea in 325 was attended by bishops from Trebizond, and also from Bichvinta (Pitiunt), the strategic port and metropolitan See situated on the border of Abkhazia. The conversion of eastern Georgia is ascribed to a slave woman from Cappadocia, Nino by name, who is credited with a number of miracles, and was a contemporary of the emperor Constantine the Great. The first Christian king of Georgia was Mirian; his tomb and that of his consort, Queen Nana, are shown to visitors in the medieval church of Samtavro in the Georgian ecclesiastical centre of Mtskheta.

GEORGIAN LITERATURE

As in Armenia, the official adoption of Christianity was followed by the introduction of a distinctive national script. The earliest Georgian inscriptions in the *Khutsuri* or priestly hand, in its uncial form, date from the fifth century. The Bible and main liturgical books were soon translated into the Georgian vernacular. By the end of the same century, a Georgian original literature was coming into being, beginning with a hagiographical masterpiece, the Martyrdom of St Shushanïk.

Georgian culture soon spread throughout the Near East and Byzantium. In the Holy Land, on Mount Sinai, on the Black Mountain near Antioch, later on Mount Athos and even in Bulgaria (at the Bachkovo monastery), diligent Georgian monks copied out their sacred texts, and acted as intermediaries between their own country and representatives of other ancient Christian civilizations.

Particularly important was the Georgian Monastery of the Holy Cross, founded by Prochorus in the eleventh century. It was here that one of the most important manuscripts in the British Library's collection (No. 136) was copied about the year 1060. By this time, the Georgians had evolved a cursive form of the priestly hand, known as *nuskhuri*.

The Georgians were also masters of the art of illumination. Unfortunately, the collection of the British Library contains no important Georgian illuminated manuscripts, and the Bodleian Library's fine Georgian collection centres on illustrated secular romances of a rather later date, for instance, the Eckstein copy of Rustaveli's epic, *The Man in the Panther's Skin*. However, the Institute of Manuscripts of the Georgian Academy of Sciences in Tbilisi has published many of its treasures in album form, including several magnificent illuminated Gospel manuscripts which rival the best Byzantine models. Other works to attract these talented and pious artists include the works of St Gregory the Theologian, the Psalms of David, and a treatise of astronomy featuring the signs of the Zodiac.

FINE ARTS

Georgian church architecture reached its apogée in the eleventh century with such masterpieces as the Cathedral of Sveti Tskhoveli in Mtskheta, Allaverdi in Kakheti province, and the Bagrat cathedral in Kutaisi, later blown up by the Turks. Fresco painting attained a high pitch of colourful realism and expressiveness.

Between the tenth and thirteenth centuries, Georgian masters created a whole series of jewelled and enamelled icons in gilt repoussé work, which rank among the masterpieces of the genre. The finest surviving specimens may be viewed in the high security chamber of the Museum of Fine Arts in Tbilisi.

CHURCH AND POLITICAL ORGANIZATION

The first head of the Georgian Church was Bishop John, sent by the emperor Constantine the Great to assist Saint Nino, about 335. The establishment of the autonomous Georgian Catholicosate is attributed to the fifth-century ruler King Vakhtang Gorgaslan. Monastic life was introduced into Georgia by a group of hermits known as the Syrian Fathers. Following the Council of Chalcedon (in 451), the Georgians at first entered the Monophysite camp, but rejoined the Orthodox fold under Archbishop Kirion I in 607. Originally, the primates of Georgia were consecrated by the Patriarchs of Antioch.

During the Crusades, the Georgians attacked the Saracens with great vigour. King David the Builder (1089–1125) and Queen Tamar (1184–1213) were renowned as champions of Christendom in the East, and Arab chroniclers described their army as 'the kernel of the religion of the Cross'.

The destiny of the medieval Georgian Church was closely linked with that of the royal Bagratid dynasty, which itself claimed descent (probably wrongly) from David and Solomon of Israel. After the annexation of Georgia by the Russian Tsar Alexander I in 1801, the Georgian Catholicos Antoni II was deposed and exiled to Russia. Only after the 1917 Revolution could the Georgian bishops, at great personal sacrifice, assemble to proclaim the restoration of the autocephaly of their ancient and glorious Church.

EARLY PRINTING IN GEORGIA

The first Georgian printed books were produced in Rome under the auspices of the

Sacra Congregatio de Propaganda Fide; the first publication of all, the Iberian Alphabet was published in 1629 (No. 137).

Within Georgia itself, the initiative was taken by King Vakhtang VI of Kartli, who set up a press in Tbilisi in 1709. Exiled Georgian princes soon after began printing Georgian texts in Moscow, where Prince Vakhushti Bagration brought out the first complete Georgian Bible in 1743 (No. 139).

136 Menologion. Parchment codex, eleventh century copied in Georgian ecclesiastical minuscules (Khutsuri, or 'priestly hand'), by the monk Black John of the Georgian Monastery of the Holy Cross near Jerusalem.

Add. 11281

This book for the commemoration of the lives of the saints represents the genre with which original Georgian literature began. A life of St Shushanik was composed about 480, and other early works include the story of the conversion of Georgia by St Nino about 330. Another saint, commemorated in the present work, was St Saba of Cappadocia who in 493 was made superior of all the hermits in Palestine by the Patriarch of Jerusalem; he was a strong supporter of theological orthodoxy.

137 Iberian Alphabet. *Alphabetum Ibericum, sive Georgianum, cum Oratione Dominicale, Salutatione Angelica, Symbolo Fidei, Praeceptis Decalogi, Ecclesiae Sacramentis et Operibus Misericordiae.* Rome, De Propaganda Fide, 1629.

621.b.4 (12)

This was the first printed book in Georgian (Iberian, in the ancient sense). Besides the description of the Georgian alphabet , the Lord's Prayer and other items are given both in Latin and Georgian. The Georgian

portion is attributed to Nicephorus the Monk, that is Nikoloz Irubak'idze-Choloqashvili.

138 Robert Bellarmine. *Dottrina Christiana breve, composta da Cardinale Bellarmino, et tradotta dal P. Bernardo Maria da Napoli . . . dalla Italiana in lingua volgare Giorgiana.* Rome, De Propaganda Fide, 1681.

G.20,004 (1)

This first substantial printed text in Georgian, is one of the apologetic works of the famous Jesuit theologian, controversialist and saint of the Counter-reformation. Cardinal Robert Bellarmine (1542–1621), among his many activities, engaged for a time in controversy with James I of England.

139 Bible. *Biblia. Ads akhali debetchduli k'art'uls enasa zeda. The Bible. Now newly printed in the Georgian tongue.* Moscow, 1743.

Or.72.d.2

This was the first printed Georgian Bible, and includes the Apocrypha, followed by a list of the Saints' Days, and a treatise on chronology. It has a preface by the Georgian ex-king Bak'ar, and a concluding discourse by the editor, Prince Vakhushti. A note in Georgian at the end of the Bible text records that this copy was the property of the Archemandrite Cyril in the year 1768.

Appendix

Oriental Christian Manuscript Bindings

Of the manuscripts discussed in this book, the earliest bindings were those produced in Egypt to cover Coptic manuscripts of the seventh and eighth centuries AD. Indeed, Coptic bindings are the oldest leather bindings known, preceding by more than five hundred years all but a handful of western manuscript bindings. From Christian Egypt, the craft of bookbinding extended to other parts of the Near and Middle East, in the wake of Islam, as it spread to Syria, Arabia and across North Africa to Spain.

The dates of bindings are sometimes difficult to determine, and may be later than the texts they enclose. The Coptic bindings are believed to be contemporary with the manuscripts themselves; but the Ethiopic texts were usually sewn and attached to their wooden boards long before the volumes were covered with leather and decorated.

The British Library collection includes some early Armenian bindings, from the tenth century onwards. Typical decoration consisted of stamped borders of stylized flowers and rope-work. Many were provided with metal clasps, and later covers often had metal ornaments, such as crucifixes, sometimes of silver filigree affixed to them.

In the following descriptions, it is the date or period of the text which has been recorded.

140 Coptic Book Cover seventh century
Fragments of a Coptic binding, originally covering papyrus boards, decorated with a geometrical design in incised and appliqué work. Two intersecting zigzag bands on the left and a diamond pattern on the right are framed by a series of vertical lines. The whole design is deeply incised. An outer border of thin strips of leather is stitched on with a leather thong, and a similar vertical strip divides the area into two unequal rectangles. An inscribed fragment of papyrus from inside the boards can be dated approximately to the seventh century. This is probably the earliest binding in the British Library.
Department of Manuscripts, Papyrus 1786 (1)

141 Coptic Book Cover seventh-eighth century
Fragment of a tooled leather cover, removed from a papyrus manuscript describing the Martyrdom of Chamoul. The binding, although damaged, shows traces of elaborate tooling, including an eight-pointed star formed of broad interlacing bands, tooled ornaments and rings. On the reverse side similar bands form an intricate zigzag interlace. Each compartment is stamped with the figure of an animal or bird.
Papyrus V

142 Coptic Book Cover seventh-eighth centuries
This splendid binding enclosed a papyrus manuscript containing the earliest known complete text of the Coptic Psalter. The leather covering, stretched over papyrus boards, is ornamented on each side with an eight-pointed star formed of broad interlacing bands. In the centre of the star is a gilded cross cut out from the leather and allowing a backing of gilded vellum to show through. Small circular figures of a goat, an eagle and a dove appear on both covers and on the flap.

The binding, which is almost certainly contemporary with the manuscript it contained (also in the British Library), dates possibly from the seventh/eighth century. It is one of the finest early Coptic bindings known.
Or.5000 (Plate 8)

143 Coptic Book Covers seventh-eighth centuries?
Elaborately decorated leather cover over thick papyrus boards. This binding was removed from an ancient papyrus manuscript of Coptic Homilies. The front cover is tooled with a zigzag interlace ornamented with small rings and crosses. The panel of the back cover is formed of interlacing bands in diamond patterns, ornamented with rings. Along the upper and lower margins are alternate figures of a dog and a bunch of grapes. The central cross is tooled with figures of a dove and four swans, or pelicans, and antelopes complete the borders of the central panel. The manuscript was written in the seventh/eighth century, and the binding may well date from the same period.
Or.5001

144 Early Islamic Binding tenth century
Plain leather covers on wooden boards. A metal pin, part of a device to hold the manuscript closed, projects from the fore-edge of the board. The sewing at the spine is protected by a strip of coarse linen pasted over it and overlapping the boards at either side. This is believed to be the earliest form of binding used for Arabic manuscripts.

The work it encloses is a Christian manuscript containing the canons of various councils of the Church, addressed to the Patriarch of Constantinople. It was written in Egypt in the tenth century.
Or.5008

145 Coptic Book Cover tenth century
Leather binding formerly enclosing a manuscript of the Martyrdom of Victor, son of Romanus, copied in AD 981. Ornamented with a rectangular frame enclosing a row of tooled stars with quatrefoils at the corners. The centre panel is marked off by tooled diagonal lines into diamond-shaped compartments containing rows of stars, quatrefoils and rings. One of the original leather thongs by which the manuscript was kept closed is intact.
Or.7022

146 Coptic Book Cover tenth century
Blind-tooled leather cover from a vellum manuscript containing part of a Discourse by Chrysostom on the Archangel Raphael, and the Apocalypse of St Paul. A variety of small binders' tools (stars, quatrefoils, circles, etc.) have been used to create an elaborate design based on a broad diagonal cross and interlacing bands, the whole contained within an ornamented rectilinear frame.
Or.7023

147 Coptic Book Cover   tenth century
Pierced and tooled leather cover from a volume of
Coptic Discourses copied in AD 987. Within the
rectilinear frame the leather has been pierced with
narrow slits to admit a strip of vellum laced in and
out, as in Or.7029. A number of holes have been
pierced in the central panel, originally to take a
white vellum backing. The central area is
ornamented with a tooled rhombus overlying a
broad diagonal cross, the spaces between being
filled with tooled figures of an animal in round
medallions. Traces of a later binding are visible on
the outer cover.

Or.7024

148 Coptic Book Covers   tenth century
Pierced and tooled leather binding from a paper
manuscript containing a history of Aaron the
Monk, copied in AD 992. A lozenge and a diagonal
cross intersect to form diamond-shaped compartments, the whole ornamented with tooled rings.
Five holes are pierced in the centre and backed
with white vellum to form a rough cross. The
rectangular frame is pierced and threaded with a
strip of white vellum.

Or.7029

149 Coptic Book Covers   tenth-eleventh century
Blind-tooled leather covers from a paper manuscript on the life of the anchorite Onuphrius,
copied in AD 1005. Within a rectangular frame a
centre panel is divided into diamond-shaped
compartments. Both frame and panel are decorated with large and small tooled stars, rings and
crosses. (Cf. No. 70, above)

Or.7027

150 Syriac Book Cover   1230
This finely tooled leather binding, contemporary
with the manuscript it contains, has been pasted
inside the upper and lower boards of the present
binding, which is probably of the nineteenth
century.

The front cover shown here is ornamented with a large
and elaborate central cross of rope-work enclosed in a
dot-punched border. Four tooled circles, with interior
ornament, occupy the four quadrants around the cross.
The whole design is enclosed within a wide and ornate
rope-work border.

The manuscript is a Gospel Lectionary of the Syrian
Church, written at Urfa (Edessa) in the monastery of

the Mother of God called Beth Aksanaya, in the year
1541 of the Greek era (AD 1230).

Or.8729

151 Syriac Binding   1475
Leather binding decorated on the front cover with
a crudely tooled cross, surrounded by borders of
rope-work and punched dots. The back cover
(shown here) consists of a central panel of rope-
work interlace within borders similar to those on
the front. An unusual and distinctive feature of
both covers is the superimposed pattern of prominent brass studs, which may have been intended to
protect the leather binding beneath. Plaited
leather straps secure the MS when closed.

A manuscript of the New Testament with various
homilies of St Ephraim and St James, Bishop of Batnān
in Serūg, written in 1475.

Or.13465

152 Ethiopian Binding   Early fifteenth century
Acts of Lālibāla of Lastā, copied before 1434,
bound in wooden boards covered with tooled
brown leather. Panels of knot-work and punched
circles decorate the border, and the centre panel
consists of a large cross enclosing a small one of
knot-work and punched circles. This is the oldest
Ethiopic MS in the British Library.

Or.719

153 Ethiopian Binding   mid-seventeenth century
Brown leather over wooden boards, decorated
with a series of narrow borders consisting of continuous stamped ornaments of various designs,
including rope-work. In the centre panel is a
tooled design of punched dots, rosettes and
double or triple lines surrounding a central cross.

This manuscript, of the Miracles of the Blessed Virgin
Mary (see No. 71, above), was copied in the reign of
Fasiladas, 1632–37.

Or.642

154 Ethiopian Binding   late-seventeenth century
Binding of brown leather stretched over wooden
boards. A small but ornate central cross, within a
larger cross flanked by tooled and punched ornaments, is surrounded by five successive tooled
borders. These display a series of stamped ornaments, each forming a continuous pattern, of
interlaced bands, rope-work, etc. The design of
the lower cover is similar.

This manuscript is entitled *Aragawi Manfasawi* or 'The Spiritual Teacher' and is followed by a work on the Fathers of the Church.

Or.762

155 Ethiopian Binding eighteenth century
Brown leather over wooden boards. The decoration consists of five successive borders, each containing a series of stamped ornaments forming a continuous pattern. A simple cross, tooled and stamped, occupies the central panel together with punched rings and tooled rectangular designs.

The manuscript enclosed in this binding describes the life and acts of Takla Haymanot, with a section on the miracles performed by him. (See No. 85, above)

Or.722

156 Ethiopian Binding Early nineteenth century
A book of magic and astrology, bound between plain wooden boards with the spine uncovered. This is an example of one of the simplest forms of binding in sections. A magical form of the cross has been scratched on both front and back covers.

Manuscript written in Ethiopic, entitled *Auda Nagast,* 'The Circle of Kings'.

Add. 16247

157 Armenian Leather Binding fifteenth century
Binding of brown leather, with a rope-work border and a tooled and stamped central panel on both upper and lower covers. A characteristically Armenian design of interlaced ribbonwork and a six-pointed star within a circle is tooled on the upper cover. Doublures of crimson brocade. The manuscript, a Sharakan or Hymnal copied in the fifteenth century, is secured with leather clasps recently renewed.

Or.5088

158 Armenian Leather Binding sixteenth century
Tooled and stamped leather binding with rectangular flap covering the fore-edge of the manuscript. Both covers are ornamented with rope-work borders, the upper one surrounding a circle of stamped tools containing a six-pointed star formed of two interlaced triangles. On the lower cover the central panel is divided into two parts containing blind-tooled ornaments, dots and rosettes. The flap is decorated with interlaced rope-work. Doublures of brocade and a leather clasp.

The manuscript, consisting of poems by Nerses the Graceful, was copied probably in the sixteenth century.

Or.2738

Concordance of Manuscript Numbers and Catalogue Entries

			Cat. No.				Cat. No.				Cat. No.
Arundel Oriental MS.		15	38	Or.	481	64		Or.	5737		130
Burney MS.		19	7		503	86			6782		46
		20	11		510	65			6796(1)		89
Cotton MS. Otho B		vi	1		515	67			6801		44
Egerton MS.		3045	15		516	66			6805		61a
		3155	17		533	68			7021		45
Harley MS.		1810	10		584	78			7022		145
		6311B	16		590	79			7023		146
Papyrus		V	141		607	77			7024		147
Papyrus		1786(1)	140		609	80			7027		149
Add.		5111	2		614	81			7029		148
		5112	8		615	82			7594		42
		7154	28		635	72			8729		150
		7169	27		641	71			8831		132
		7170	29		642	153			8833		125
		7174	31		645	73			9046		33
		11281	136		649	74			9271		43
		11856	37		685	83			11264		124
		11870	5		687–8	84			11370		102
		12134	23		718	88			11602		94
		12139	25		719	152			11764		96
		14425	19		721	85			11804		99
		14429	24		722	155			12025		91
		14438	21		762	154			12550		133
		14445	20		790	69			12859		97, 98
		14451	18		818	87			12959		92
		14591	22		1316	49			13156		70
		15411	119		1317	50			13227		93
		16247	156		2668	123			13465		151
		17983	30		2707	128			13654		112
		18549	114		2738	158			13804		118
		19352	4		3372	26			13808		134
		24188	75, 76		3716C	100		Bodleian Library			
		27301	131		4410	32		Armenian MS.	D 3		116
		37002	12		5000	142			D 4		121
		39584	9		5001	143			E 1		127
		39603	6		5008	144		Bodleian Library Hunt	17		47
		39626	13		5088	157		Chester Beatty Library MS.	551		129
		39627	14		5304	122			558		113
		40731	3		5423	90, 95			559		117
	Or.	81	111		5464	48			561		120
		480	63		5626	114			602		126

Suggestions for further reading

AZIZ S. ATIYA. *A History of Eastern Christianity.* London, 1968. (An extensive treatment of the non-Chalcedonian Churches of the East, with maps and bibliography.)

H. BUCHTAL AND O. KURZ. *A Handlist of Illuminated Oriental Christian Manuscripts.* London, 1942. (The material described relates to the Byzantine era, and includes numerous references to the manuscripts included in the present volume.)

H. J. GOODACRE AND A. P. PRITCHARD, compilers. *Guide to the Department of Oriental Manuscripts and Printed Books.* London, 1977. (Contains brief descriptions of the collections by language, with bibliographical descriptions of the various catalogues of Oriental Manuscripts.)

T. G. H. JAMES, A. F. SHORE AND I. E. S. EDWARDS. *A General Introductory Guide to the Egyptian Collections in the British Museum.* London, 1964. (See especially Chapter 8, on Roman and Christian Egypt.)

E. KITZINGER. *Early Medieval Art in the British Museum.* London, 2nd. edn., 1955.

D. M. LANG, ed. *Guide to Eastern Literatures.* London, 1971. (Includes articles by A. K. Irvine on Ethiopic, and D. M. Lang on Armenian and Georgian.)

D. T. RICE. *Art of the Byzantine Era.* London, 1963. (With numerous illustrations, and bibliography; includes chapters on Oriental Christian Art.)

E. ULLENDORF. *Ethiopia and the Bible.* The Schweich Lectures of the British Academy, 1967. London, 1968.

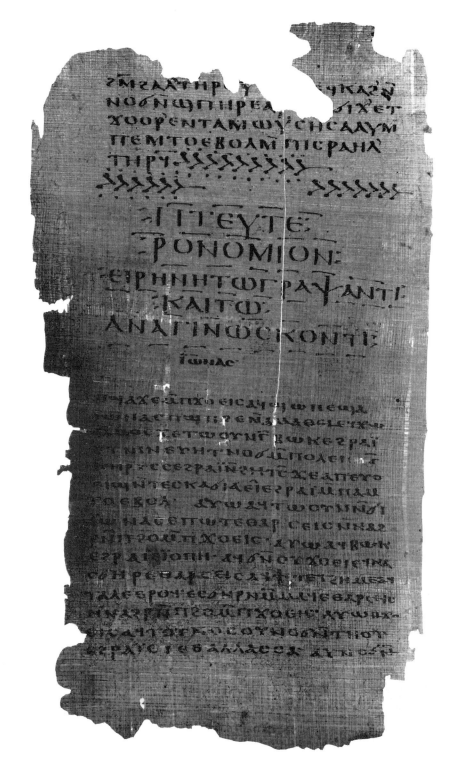

1 Deuteronomy, Jonah and Acts. Coptic, early fourth century. Deut. 24.11–end, and Jonah 1.1–4.
Add. 7594, f. 53a. (Cat. no. 42)

2 Pentateuch, Syriac, AD 463. Peshitta version, Genesis 29.25–30.2. Add. 14425, f. 31a. (Cat. no. 19)

3 Curetonian Gospels. Syriac, fifth century. John 6.53–64. Add. 14451, f. 49b. (Cat. no. 18)

4   Canon Tables. Greek, seventh century. Add. 5111, f. 11a. (Cat. no. 2)

5 St John the Evangelist. Greek. Late twelfth century. Add. 5112, f. 134. (Cat. no. 8)

6 Sianfu Nestorian Inscription. Chinese and Syriac, AD 781. Rubbing in the Department of Oriental
Manuscripts and Printed Books. 15406. a.6, 11 and 35. (Cat. no. 34)

7 St Menas on horseback. Miracles of St Menas, and Canon Texts. Nubian, ninth century. Or. 6805, f. 10a.
(Cat. no. 61a)

8   Leather Binding. Homilies. Coptic, seventh–eighth centuries. Or. 5000. (Cat. no. 142)

9 St Mark the Evangelist. Four Gospels. Coptic, AD 1173. Bodleian Library, Hunt MS no. 17, f. 120b.
(Cat. no. 47)

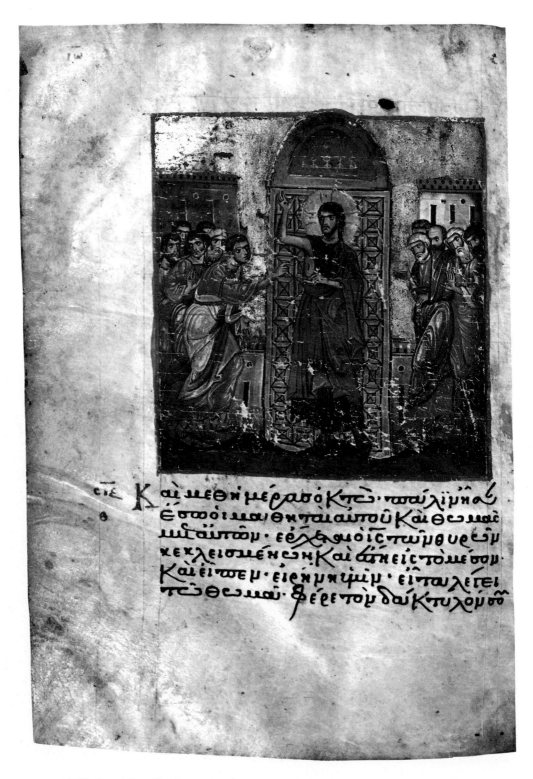

10 The Incredulity of St Thomas. Four Gospels. Greek, first quarter of the thirteenth century. Harley MS no. 1810, f. 261b. (Cat. no. 10)

11 Title page of St Mark's Gospel. Awag Vänk Gospels. Armenian, AD 1200. Or. 13654, f. 117a.
(Cat. no. 112)

12 St Mark the Evangelist. Four Gospels. Armenian, AD 1321. Add. 15411, f. 91b. (Cat. no. 119)

13 Heading of St Mark's Gospel, with a miniature of the Blessed Virgin Mary. Add. 15411, f. 92a.
(Cat. no.119)

14 The Falling Asleep of the Blessed Virgin Mary; and the Deesis, or Exaltation of the Cross, by Toros. Armenian, AD 1311. Dublin, Chester Beatty Library, Armenian MS no. 559. (Cat. no. 117)

15 St Mark the Evangelist by the illuminator Sargis Picak. Four Gospels. Armenian, AD 1329.
Dublin, Chester Beatty Library, Armenian MS no. 561. (Cat. no. 120)

16 The Metropolitan Jacob. Serres Gospels. Slavonic, AD 1354–5. Add. 39626, f. 292b. (Cat. no. 13)

17 St John Chrysostom. Leitourgikon from Brusa. Greek, AD 1644. Egerton MS no. 3155. (Cat. no. 17)

18 St Gregory the Illuminator, and King Tiridates of the Armenians. Menologion. Armenian, AD 1489.
Dublin, Chester Beatty Library, Armenian MS no. 602. (Cat. no. 126)

19 Khachkar, or an Armenian Stone Cross. Armenia, thirteenth century. (Cat. no. 110)

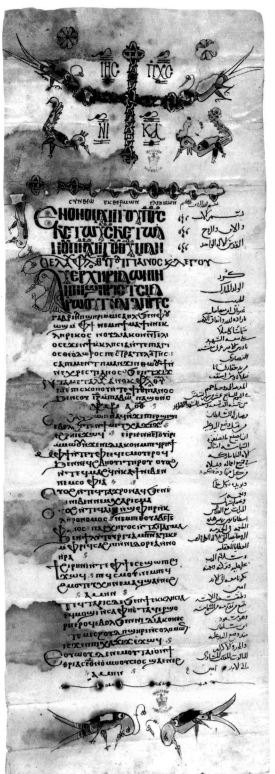

20 The Orders of a Deacon. Document from Akhmim, Upper Egypt.
Coptic and Arabic, AD 1363. Or. 5464. (Cat. no. 48)

21 Chapter Heading from a Psalter. Arabic, Naskhi hand, with Coptic glosses, sixteenth century.
Arundel Orient MS no. 15, f. 38b. (Cat. no. 38)

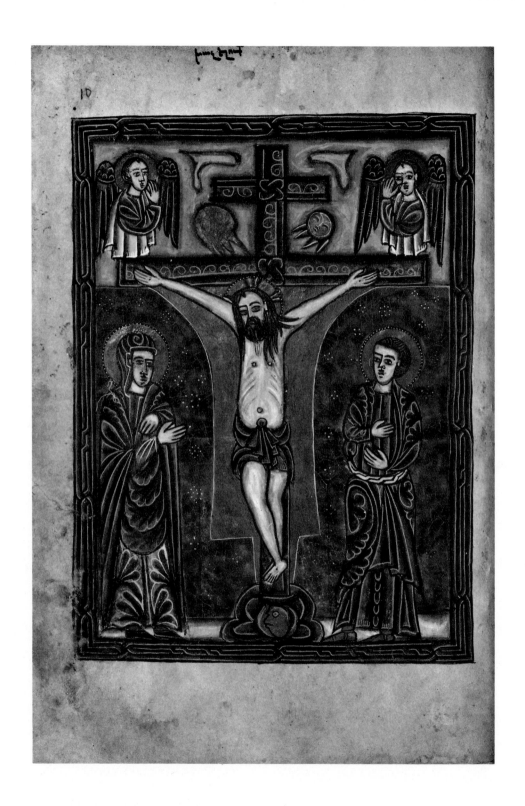

22 The Crucifixion. Four Gospels. Armenian, AD 1607. Or. 5737, f. 10b. (Cat. no. 130)

23 The Annunciation; and the Adoration of the Magi. Menologion. Armenian, AD 1653.
Or. 12550, f. 257b. (Cat. no. 133)

فوقف يسوع ودعاهما وقال لهما ما تريدان ان افعل بكما
قالا له يا رب ان تفتح اعيننا فتحنن يسوع ولمس اعينهما
وللوقت ابصرا وانفتحت اعينهما وتبعـــاه ❊

الفصل السادس والستون

ولما قربوا من يروشليم وجاوا الى بيت فاجي قريب جبل
الزيتون حينئذ ارسل يسوع اثنين من تلاميذه وقال
لهما ان هبا الى القريه الة امامكما فتجدان اتانا مربوطة
وجحشا معها فحلاهما واتياني بهما فان قال كلما احد شيـا
فقولا ان الرب محتاج اليهما فهو يرسلهما للوقت ❊ كان
هذا ليتم ما قيل في النبي القايل قولوا لابنـة صهيون
هاهوذا ملكك ياتيك متواضعا راكبا على اتان

وحش

24 Christ healing Two Blind Men. Four Gospels, Arabic. Printed in Rome, AD 1590–91. With Tempesta's
woodcuts, after Dürer. Or. 70.d.6. (Cat. no. 41)

ማቴዎስ፡

ዘክመ፡ፈ፡ወዕሙ፡እግዚ፡እነ፡ለ፤፡ዕ፡ው፡ራን፡

ወይቤልዎ፡እግዚእ፡ክ
ሙ፡ይትከሠታ፡አዕይን
ቲነ፡ወአምሐርዎ፡ለእ
ግዚእ፡ኢየሱከ፡ወመሐ
ርሙ፡እግዚእ፡ኢየሱክ፡

ወገሠሦሙ፡ወለከፎሙ፡
አዕይንቲሆ፡ሙ፡ቀወደቤ
ሎሙ፡በከሙ፡ሃይማኖ
ትክሙ፡ወአሚና፡ትክሙ፡
ይኩንክሙ፡ቀወበጊዜሃ፡

ነጽሩ፡ሶቤሃ፡ወተከሠት፡
አዕይንቲሆሙ፡ወርእ
ዩ፡ሶቤሃ፡ወተለውዎ፡ቀ

✦   ✦   ✦   ✦

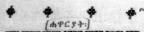
ሐዋርያት፡

25 Christ healing Two Blind Men. Four Gospels, copied by Takla Maryam. Ethiopic, AD 1665.
Or. 510, f. 51a. (Cat. no. 65)

26 The Virgin and Child. Miracles of the Blessed Virgin Mary. Ethiopic, mid-seventeenth century.
Or. 641, f. 180a. (Cat. no. 71)

27 St Luke the Evangelist. Four Gospels. Coptic and Arabic, AD 1663. Or. 1316, f. 111b. (Cat. no. 49)

28 The Abuna (or Archbishop) Takla Haymanot enthroned. Degua, an Ethiopic Hymnary, AD 1735.
Or. 584, f. 155a. (Cat. no. 78)

ወሰስ ትዮ ደረደሩ፡ እን ዘ ፰ ፬ ፪ ወቦ ወ ድ የ ን ዮ ዋ ዕ ት፡
ወ ፸ ፱ ዓ ፡ ለ ጌ ቶ ፱ ደ ፡ ዘ አ ሠ ር ፣ የ ፡ በ ኃ ለ ሉ ይ ፨

29 The Abuna Yared. Or. 584, f. 232a. (Cat. no. 78)

30 Noah's Ark. Tabiba Tabiban, an Ethiopic Hymnary, eighteenth century. Or. 590, f. 8b. (Cat. no. 79)

31 The Emperor, Yekuno Amlak (reigned AD 1270–85), receiving Muslim Ambassadors. Isaiah, Daniel and Apocryphal Books. Ethiopic, late eighteenth century. Or. 503, ff. 75b–76a. (Cat. no. 86)

32 Processional Cross, with interlaced patterns and inscription. Ethiopic, sixteenth century. British Museum, Department of Medieval and Later Antiquities. (Cat. no. 104a)